KT-482-397

"HERE COME THE GLASGOW KEELIES!"

Collected and edited
by Lorne A. Wallace

published by

*Dunning
Parish
Historical
Society*

Lino-cut illustrations by Albie Sinclair
Maps by Ken Laing

Published by the Dunning Parish Historical Society
Old Schoolhouse,
Newton of Pitcairns,
Dunning, Perthshire PH2 0SL

ISBN-0-9536837-0-2

Scanning, typesetting and printing
by Nevisprint Ltd., Fort William, Inverness-shire

Contents

Introduction

Uprooted from their homes in the east end of Glasgow and separated from their families for the first time in their lives, almost three hundred evacuees stepped on to the platform of Dunning Station, Perthshire. It was about 4 pm on September 3, 1939, the Sunday Britain declared war on Germany. They were weary after a journey of several hours in a train without corridors or toilets. A few fortunate children had their mothers with them, others had brothers or sisters, many had only school pals. The children were mostly pupils at Haghill School and several teachers accompanied the group.

The village to which they were to be bussed lay two miles to the south, an out of the way community, declined to half the size of its heyday as a centre for handloom weaving and agricultural fairs. Now it lay in the economic shadow of Perth, eight miles north-east, a quiet place where many of the residents had never taken as long a journey as their new visitors had just experienced.

The war with Germany had been long anticipated. The children coming to Dunning were a tiny fraction of the participants in a massive government scheme to evacuate city children thought to be in danger of bombing to the comparative safety of rural Britain. The official evacuation scheme was voluntary yet involved some three and a half million people across the nation. Dunning, like other country places, would also receive children evacuated privately by their families as well as a second wave of official and private evacuees when the serious bombing began.

Many years later, as a Canadian transplanted to my mother's birthplace of Dunning, I heard of the evacuees who had come to Dunning. My wife and I had fallen in love with the village. I had become interested in Dunning's history, had published a book of old photographs about the village and started a local history society.

But what was this about so many evacuees to this one small place? As a schoolboy in Winnipeg, I could remember an evacuee from Liverpool in my class, Edna Pitcher, and my chums and I had often wondered what had become of her. There had been perhaps a handful of other British evacuees in our big primary school. Now I became curious about the crowd of evacuees who must have swamped Dunning: who were they, what kind of experiences had they had and what sort of impact had the evacuation made on their lives? And what impact did they have on Dunning and its people?

With the help of Les McColl, the one evacuee we knew of and who still lived in the village, we managed to locate a few others. It took months. My background was in broadcasting, and with the help of equipment and pupils from Auchterarder High School, we made a little video programme about Dunning evacuees to show at an Historical Society meeting.

From the making of that video sprang the idea of an Evacuees' Reunion. It was coming up to 1994, fifty-five years after the arrival of the evacuees. With the help of several evacuees and spouses---Les and Ina McColl, Lily and Walter King, George and Helen Boardman, Betty Bridgeford---the Dunning Parish Historical Society planned the first Evacuees' Reunion which any of us had ever heard of. It then took more painstaking work to locate evacuees to whom we could send invitations.

Finally, on the weekend of Friday, September 3, 1994, the Reunion took place. It began in the playground at Dunning Primary school, to where the evacuees had been bussed from Dunning Station fifty-five years before. The ex-evacuees, thirty to forty of them, wore replicas of gas mask boxes and had name labels tied to their jackets. National and local television, radio and print media were there to record the billeting of the evacuees in the homes of Historical Society members, just as they had been billeted with strangers fifty-five years before.

Then the ex-evacuees visited classes at Dunning and five other nearby schools from Forgandenny to Blackford to tell pupils about their experiences as evacuees. The Society held an evening get-together with further onstage reminiscences. With much visiting and socialising the next day, the Reunion climaxed in the Village Hall in a glorious Big Band Dance, with Ron Spiers' 16 piece band playing music dating to World War II.

A year later, September 3, 1995, in an event organised by evacuees led by George Boardman and Lily King, the Rev. Alan Roy conducted a special church service in Dunning Parish Church. The evacuees then proceeded through Dunning to unveil a plaque, subscribed by the evacuees, on the wall of St. Serf's Church. It reads "This plaque is dedicated to the villagers of Dunning from the evacuees, mostly from Glasgow, of the Second World War, 1939-1945. 'A Welcome Was Made and Not Forgotten', 3rd September, 1995."

After the unveiling, evacuees and Society members met in the Village Hall, and we had a chance to meet evacuees who had not come the previous year. With journalistic zeal I recorded interviews with them, as I had begun doing a year before to capture stories which would shortly be lost forever.

From Les McColl and several others, we had already heard about how the local children had sometimes jeered at the newcomers, calling them "Glasgow keelies", slang meaning something like "city toughs" or "hooligans". In retaliation the Glaswegians had called the locals "teuchters", by which they meant " hicks" or "country bumpkins".

As the interviews accumulated, a different picture than the one I had read about before, of poor slum kids lucking out in the country, began to emerge. In fact, it seemed many children from Glasgow came to an environment often lacking the facilities they were accustomed to.

What most impressed me was the varied nature of their experiences. To help round out the picture, I interviewed people who as children had not been part of the official evacuation but had been evacuated privately. I obtained material from teachers. I also talked with Dunning people who remembered the evacuees. And to add another dimension, I talked to present village residents whose evacuee experiences had taken place elsewhere.

From these interviews, wonderful stories often unfolded. We weren't just gathering details of local history, we were gaining insights into the lives of participants in one of the great early dramas of World War II.

Several of those whom we interviewed have died. That somehow makes it all the more important not to have these stories languish in an archive, but to share them now.

"Here Come the Glasgow Keelies!" is dedicated to all the boys and girls who came to Dunning as evacuees, and to the villagers who welcomed them.

September 3, 1994. Scenes at the first Dunning Evacuees' Reunion

Acknowledgments

This book owes everything to the many evacuees who have been willing over the last five years to be interviewed in person or to jot down their memories, and to all those who have loaned precious photographs.

The Dunning Parish Historical Society, which has undertaken publication of the book, is a remarkable organisation. Based in a community of only 1,000 population, the Society has over 250 members, local and postal, and has earned a reputation as being "incredibly active" (the Strathearn Herald). In its brief seven years' existence the Historical Society has undertaken such varied ventures as an art show, museum exhibitions, barn dances, archaeological fieldwalks, a flower festival, the setting up of a fine website *(www.dunning.mcmail.com)*, and of course, evacuees' reunions. Publishing a full-length book is a new enterprise involving certain risks, and I am grateful for the enthusiastic support given by the Society committee and members.

Gathering the material for the book has been a great personal pleasure for me, allowing me to meet many interesting people, some of whom have become friends. The interviewing was the fun part.

When it came to sorting out material for the book, the work began, and for help with that I am indebted to several individuals.

Throughout the project, my mainstay has been my wife Patricia. Her keen critical eye, judgement, personal sacrifices of time and space, and assistance in a thousand other ways have been vital.

I'm also indebted for research, information, material and editorial advice to several other kind people: Walter Perrie, Elizabeth Fletcher, Simon Warren, Finella Wilson, Margaret Graham, Al Fairbairn, Hamish MacEwen, Bill Wanless, Graham Bell, Ted Dorsett, Angus Howie, Shona Sinclair, David Wilson, Louis Flood, Photographers, and the staff of the Archives, Reference and Local Studies departments of the A.K. Bell Library, Perth. And special thanks must go to two generous friends: Albie Sinclair for his fine lino-cuts, and Kenny Laing for his made to order maps.

Lorne Wallace, Dunning, 1999

*(Above) The Big Band dance at the first Evacuees Reunion, 1994
and
(Below) the evacuees parade from their church service, September 3, 1995*

Glossary

accumulator	a rechargeable electric cell
Anderson shelter	an outdoor World War II air raid shelter, usually in a garden
ATC	Air Training Corps
Beano	a popular comic paper
bit, **half bit**	the portion of a potato drill assigned to be picked by an individual--smaller children often had half bits
black lead	a metal polish made of graphite
bothy, bothies	a one room building in which (farm) labourers are lodged
burn	a small stream, a creek
called up	summoned to serve in the military
creel	a basket for carrying potatoes, etc.
crocodile	line of schoolchildren in pairs
doublers	a children's ball game
The Dragon	(pron. dray'-gun) the part and street of Dunning properly called Newton of Pitcairns. (Dragon comes from the legend that St. Serf slew a dragon there)
drill	a row, as of potatoes
dry toilet	a lavatory in which faeces and urine drop into a pail
dungarees	overalls
gird	a wheel or hoop hit along with a stick
guddle	to catch fish with the hands by groping under stones or the banks of a stream
howking	e.g. tattie-howking means the harvesting of potatoes
itchy coo	prickly seed e.g. of the dog-rose which children put down each other's backs

keelie	a pejorative term meaning rough young working class people from the city.
lifting	digging potatoes
loo	informal word for toilet
Luftwaffe	German air force
manse	the house provided for a parish minister
marcel wave	a kind of deep wave in the hair
messages	one's shopping, provisions, an errand
mod cons	modern conveniences
Morrison shelter	an air raid shelter placed inside houses
NAAFI	Navy Army and Air Force Institutes: canteens for servicemen
National Service	compulsory service in the national armed forces
neeps	turnips (swedes)
Nissen hut	tunnel-shaped hut of corrugated iron, cement-floored
nit	egg or young form of louse
outwith	Scottish term meaning outside, beyond
palliasse	a straw mattress
pantaloons	overalls
pend	a passageway between houses or leading into the back of a block of houses
Phoney War	period following the declaration of war when no serious bombing was done on Britain
potato/tattie dressing	uncovering and cleaning potatoes which have been stored in earth covered pits
RAF	Royal Air Force

riddle	coarse sieve for cleaning corn etc.
shawing	cutting the tops off vegetables e.g. turnips
sheepdip	a liquid chemical used in a bath to kill harmful insects in a sheep's coat
skull or scull	a shallow basket for gathering potatoes etc.
spate	a river-flood e.g. the burn is in spate
tatties	potatoes
tawse	a leather punishment strap with thongs, used in schools
tenement	a large building of three or more storeys divided into flats for separate households
teuchter	a contemptuous term meaning a countrified person, a hick
thrawn	obstinate, contrary
threshing mill	a machine once used to separate grain from straw
tied house	a dwelling occupied by someone subject to his working for the owner
V1	a German rocket bomb, nicknamed doodle-bug, used against Britain from June 15, 1944, launched from France. The attacks stopped on September 1, 1944, when the Allies overran the launching area
V2	a German rocket weapon, higher powered than the V1, which began falling on Britain September 8, 1944, launched from the Netherlands. The last V2 fell March 28, 1944.
wally close	a tiled entry to a tenement
wellies	(wellingtons) rubber boots, usually knee high

A class at Haghill School, Denistoun, in the east end of Glasgow, just prior to the war.

The Big Influx

Leaving Glasgow

Chapter 1: I ONLY WANTED TWO!

On the day war was declared, nearly three hundred evacuees from Glasgow descended on the wee Perthshire village of Dunning, the Perthshire Advertiser reported. Among the evacuees were Ron Freeland and his two sisters Margaret and Lily. Here are Ron and Lily's memories of that day, and those of Mrs. Agnes Hurry and her daughter Nancy, with whom the Freelands were billeted.

Ron Freeland, now of Culloden: As war-clouds gathered during the last week of August, 1939, parents who had agreed to the Evacuation Scheme received notice about their children's departure. Pupils at Haghill Primary School, Denistoun, in east Glasgow, would leave by train on Sunday morning, September third for unannounced country destinations. Some other Glasgow schools left even earlier on September first and second.

The government's plan was that parents should be given the option of sending their children out of the big cities to the comparative safety of the countryside. This was after seeing on newsreels the horrors of the indiscriminate bombing by the German Air Force, the Luftwaffe, of many Spanish towns, Guernica in particular, during the 1936-39 Spanish Civil War. A great many innocent civilians were killed or maimed. If war broke out it was expected that Glasgow, with her factories and shipyards, would be a prime target for enemy bombers, along with other big British cities.

On September first, German armies invaded Poland and two days later, having received no reply to its demands that they withdraw, Great Britain declared war against Germany. This was to honour a pact which we had made with France to aid Poland should she be attacked.

At 11 o'clock on the Sunday morning, as Prime Minister Neville Chamberlain issued the Declaration of War, I found myself with my two younger sisters and a few hundred other children awaiting the arrival at Alexandra Park Station of a train which would transport us to our still unknown destination.

Lily Freeland (now Mrs. King of Cumbernauld): My memory of evacuation day began on Walter Street. Everybody was leaning out the windows waving, as we went in a crocodile of children down to Haghill School.

We had each been given a label attached with a string, and on it was written our name and address and what they called the section number, which was the part of the playground you had to go to. We were clutching bags of sandwiches because it was going to be a long time to get to wherever we were going---we weren't told. We had our gas masks slung diagonally, to make sure we had our hands free so we could show our label and clutch our sandwiches in the other hand.

I remember my mother and father at the gates. They didn't come into the playground but stood outside waving to us. To me it was heart-rending, because I was only five. I didn't know why I was going away. I was with my brother and sister who were a bit older than me and who were to take care of me, but I had a funny feeling about leaving mum and dad. It was the first time I'd been away without them. I think I cried most of the time. I had a feeling that I was being sent away because I had done something wrong. In no way did I connect being evacuated with a war.

Ron Freeland: We clambered aboard, clutching our small suitcases. Across our chests, attached with a loop of string, hung square cardboard boxes containing gas masks. These had been issued to us a few weeks before at school, when we were instructed by visiting officials on air raid precautions.

It was feared the enemy might use poison gas as they had done during the 1914-18 War.

Each compartment on the train held a teacher or a lady helper to keep us in order. There must have been children from other schools too: I seem to remember a few stops at stations on the way, when groups of children would disembark with their teachers. At the end of a long, long journey, or so it seemed to us, we reached Dunning Station where two or three buses waited to transport us the final two miles to the village.

Lily (Freeland) King: I only vaguely remember the train journey. I think I wept buckets, being upset too by the sight of all the other children who were crying, even older ones who knew what it was all about. Because…although it was quiet and calmly done, there was a feeling…well, mums and dads conveyed a panic, a frightened feeling. They were obviously afraid that the minute war was declared bombs were going to start falling. So the quicker they could get the children away from Glasgow, the better.

Ron Freeland: I seem to recall the evacuees lined up in the hall while Dunning people passed along the line choosing the child, or children, they would agree to take into their homes.

A few of these local people were farmers and I recall one burly man of the soil calling out that he wanted six boys! He chose the six biggest lads he could find among us. I expect he found plenty for them to do on his farm. My next-door neighbour and pal from back home, George Boardman, was one of the six who set off to Easter Clevage farm.

Although I was over 12 years old I was a rather small slightly-built lad. But I was still "big brother" to my two younger sisters, Margaret (aged 8) and Lily (aged 5) who clung tightly to my hands. I was determined not to lose sight of them, and I'd promised my mother and father to take good care of them.

Lily (Freeland) King: It was Mrs. Agnes Hurry who came to pick up our family. But she had come with the express wish of taking two girls. She already had a young daughter, Nancy, and she thought it would be nice to have two wee girls staying with her. She was all for taking my sister Margaret and myself. But Ronald, my brother, had been given the job of looking after his sisters. Taking his duties very seriously, he wasn't going to let us go without him. So he said "All or nothing", and Mrs. Hurry, who was a very kind-hearted lady, said, "Oh, I'll have the boy along too".

Mrs. Agnes Hurry

Mrs. Agnes Hurry: I can't really remember who it was that gave us the instructions, maybe Mr. McKinnon, the minister of St. Serf's Church, but we had to go down to the school, and the evacuees were all there.

They just started to give them to people who would take them, the people who were there. I was thinking of taking two girls, because I had a little girl.

They gradually got fewer and fewer, and I was well down the list. I only wanted two, two girls. But I got three---there were these three left, two girls and their brother.

Nancy Hurry: The day the evacuees came, I was just five. I can remember going up to mum's friend's house. Dad came up later and took me home. And I was all right until he told me there was a boy in the family, and then I cried. I didn't want a boy! And I don't really remember much more about it.

Lily (Freeland) King: Later on that night, because I remember being in pyjamas, all bathed and all ready for bed, the door went and who should come in but…my mum!

Mrs. Agnes Hurry: So I got three, plus the mother. They were all here and up in the house, and I had them bathed and ready for bed by the time she arrived. She actually got lost in transit.

Lily (Freeland) King: My mum had refused to let us go off on our own, and had wangled herself in as a helper for evacuees. This must have been almost a snap decision because there was no plan to go with us or to join us. That same day she must have got home, sat down with my dad, and asked him would it be all right and then made some sort of arrangement with the authorities, who would likely still be at Haghill School, for her and Mrs. Boardman, (George's mother), to join us through at Dunning, They took a bus to Dunblane. There they found a bus to Dunning; because it was complicated getting to Dunning then by road.

Ron Freeland: You can imagine the reunion. Mr. and Mrs. Hurry agreed to allow us the use of their two attic bedrooms until we could find some accommodation of our own. It was to be into the new year before this came about. Meantime we were accepted almost as members of this family, living in extremely comfortable surroundings with plenty of good, wholesome food.

Top: Ron Freeland,
Centre: L. Mrs. Freeland,
R. Mrs. Boardman
Bottom: L. Lily, R Margaret Freeland.

We were treated with great kindness and consideration.

Mrs. Agnes Hurry: That was the start of it, and we had them for sixteen weeks I think it was. I was quite pleased with the evacuees. We were very lucky, we got a very nice family. Some of them were terrible, they had to do all sorts of things for their heads. Terrible, some of them.

It was so funny, Lily's father was a grocer and my husband was a grocer, we lived above our grocer's shop. They were a nice family.

People that had evacuees, they seemed to get along fine, after they got them sorted out and cleaned up. And really, I never heard anyone complaining about the evacuees.

We just got on with it. I quite enjoyed it. It was a lot of work, certainly, when there were eight of us in the house to cook for. But I managed, and then the family got a house in the village, to be on their own, which was nice for them too.

Ron Freeland: After breakfast I helped Mr. Hurry load his van with groceries, which he delivered to farms, bothies and other customers outwith the village two or three days each week. I accepted his offer to accompany him on these trips with great enthusiasm. Arrangements for our schooling hadn't yet been finally agreed and for the next few weeks I like to think I was of some help.

I'll never forget the day I paid my first visit to a bothy. With a basket of groceries on my arm I lifted the latch of the door and walked in. The workers, of course, were all out at various jobs around the farm. Approaching the table on which I had been instructed to leave the supplies, I was horrified to see a large number of mice scurrying off. I had apparently disturbed them enjoying breakfast from the leftovers which littered the table. I couldn't get out of that place quickly enough!

Lily (Freeland) King: When we lived with Mrs. Hurry, my mum helped with the cleaning and also worked up at the Manse where the minister and his wife, Mr. & Mrs. McKinnon, had taken in several evacuees. My mother and Mrs. Boardman helped with the evacuees, keeping them clean and washing hair. They had a fetish about clean heads. We had to have our hair washed an awful lot of times.

In school we were visited by a nurse, practically every second week. Even when we were finally integrated with the Dunning children, we evacuees were called out one by one to have our heads examined. Not in front of other children---we were taken into another room to be examined. To me it wasn't a nice thing. I was ashamed. My family were all clean, we had never had any trouble, we were always shampooed and washed every night practically, and having a nurse examine your head…it was obviously nits. It must have been something that Glasgow children brought as a tiny extra. But I didn't take to this fortnightly inspection of us evacuees!

I do see it now, because they were taking in children from homes all over Glasgow, not all from homes like ours.

Ron Freeland: My mother, sisters and I moved from the Hurrys' to rented rooms in a terraced house on Perth Road. Then after 2 or 3 years we moved to the lower apartments in the Commercial Buildings (the former Commercial Hotel) on Auchterarder Road. After leaving school on turning fifteen, I worked full-time with Mrs. Hurry in the family shop, doling out the weekly rations. If I remember correctly the coupons in your ration-book allowed you one egg per week and 1 lb. of jam per month. These amounts, with/lb. meat from the butcher's, augmented by sausage & haggis, varied only slightly through the war years.

Lily (Freeland) King: It took a while to integrate, it took a while to get to know people because Dunning was very isolated. People all knew each other, had known each other all their lives, and it must have been as difficult for them as it was for us. They knew nothing about us. We had different accents: Glasgow accents were even more different then: we've become more cosmopolitan with the television now. We didn't always get on awfully well with the Dunning children. There were many scrapes, especially among the older children. Us wee ones weren't aware enough to bother. We all just played together.

Nancy Hurry: I think looking back there might have been a sense of difference between local children and evacuees. There might have been this feeling on our part that there was something different about them, but then they were all quite able to stand up for themselves! Because they came from the big town, you see. I think some of them wondered where the picture house was and the chip shops. But they soon got used to it.

When the Freelands moved to their own house, I went along and played with Lily. Her older sister, she drew little figures and dresses for us, and we used to dress these paper dolls.

Ron Freeland: On the night of Friday, 13 March, 1941, occurred an event which will remain forever etched in my memory. That evening it seemed that the whole of the Luftwaffe was flying over our village. For over an hour and a half no fewer that ninety-six waves, each of four or five planes, passed over, their ominous drone which always seemed peculiar to German aircraft engines and whose sound was always instantly recognised by those of us who lived through the war, brought a chill of fear to the hearts of us below. This huge armada flew in over the North Sea, crossing the coast below Aberdeen then turning south right down Strathearn (where we were) to their main targets of Glasgow and Clydebank. Damage and casualties there were considerable. The BBC announced next day that extensive fires were still burning. My older sister Jean travelled up to Dunning the next weekend and was able to recount to us the horrors of that terrible night. The blitz continued the very next night as the raiders returned to the same areas.

Nancy Hurry: I can remember the night one of Ron Freeland's friends, George Boardman, came belting into the house in a great state to tell us that Italy had surrendered. It meant nothing to me but obviously was of great excitement to them.

Looking back, I suppose it must have been quite difficult for some of the evacuees. I think they were well enough looked after in the homes they went to, but I don't know. Maybe it wasn't all sweetness and light for the kids, I've no idea. It must have been quite a shock. Lily had her mother and her brother and sister, but I don't know about those who didn't have parents: I don't think it would have been very cheery for them at all. I certainly wouldn't have liked to experience it myself, I can assure you.

Ron Freeland: A regular feature of village life was the Friday or Saturday evening concert held in the village hall. These were very well attended by the soldiers billeted here and by villagers and there was rarely a lack of volunteers willing to do a turn: singing, dancing, sketches or monologues. One performer always in great demand was my sister, Margaret, who although only 11 or 12 years, was a seasoned trouper, having appeared with a concert party back home in Glasgow. At the end of these concerts the hall was cleared of benches and chairs and the grown-ups would then enjoy themselves dancing, on into the wee hours, music being supplied by a small local band led by accordionist Bob Malcolm.

In March, 1942, my friend Bud Sharples and I joined the Air Training Corps in Auchterarder. Although the age of admission was 15 years, we were both accepted a few months short of that. One of the CO's greatest ambitions was to form a pipe-band and Gordon and I enrolled as drummers.

9

Ron Freeland's beloved Air Training Corps, Auchterarder

My pipe-band tuition stood me in good stead when I was asked by Bob Malcolm to join his dance-band as its drummer. We played for dances in Dunning Hall, also for the neighbouring communities in Auchterarder, Gask, Forteviot and Forgandenny. For an evening's work, usually from 7:30 pm till 2 am, we were paid the sum of one pound each. This was really good money considering that as a 16-year-old, I was at that time earning 15/- for a full week's work as a grocer. This dance-band fee, however, was well earned when one considers we had to rely on cycling to reach the various venues. This with our instruments strapped to our backs!

Lily (Freeland) King: Looking back at it, I was very happy here in Dunning. It was a marvellous thing to think that I had green grass and open spaces, and there was no fear of traffic. My first five years were in a Glasgow tenement, and the only place we had to play was a park and it was over a very busy main road. So it was often a case of playing in the back court or on the street, but we weren't ragamuffin children, we weren't dirty, we had plenty of games to play.

Coming to Dunning opened up a whole new kind of life. It made my early years very happy. My war years were spent with really no connection with the war, other than when the soldiers came and were billeted here. The war didn't really mean anything to me. But Dunning has an awful special place in my heart.

*Margaret, Lily and Mrs. Jean Freeland
in Dunning, 1939*

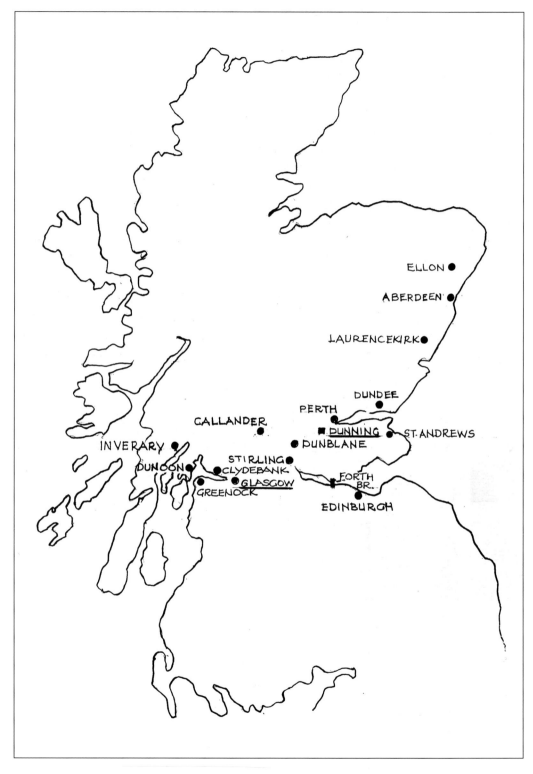

Scotland and the Dunning evacuees

Chapter 2: AS THE LOCALS SAW IT

Kenny Laing was born in Dunning in July 1922. He was asked to help with the arrival of the evacuees in Dunning on September 3, 1939.

Ken Laing: I was working in Perth, an apprentice architect by that time. My old headmaster, Mr. Benzies, came to me and said they required some people down at Dunning School to do odd jobs when the evacuees arrived. All the organisation for the arrival of the children had been pre-arranged.

Sunday morning, Mr. Chamberlain came on the radio and said we were at war with Germany, so everyone knew the operation would be put in hand. Mr. Benzies seemed to be in charge, since it was all to take place at the school, but my recollections aren't that good. I was young, only a teenager.

My recollection is that we went down about midday. As children came in by bus from the train station they would be allocated to either one of the two open playsheds which stood back to back in the centre of the schoolground. I was assigned to one of the sheds to receive the children and ferry them into the school.

Kenny Laing at 17

It was a warmish quite pleasant day, as I recall, and the children began arriving about three or four o'clock. They had to come from Glasgow by train, and as I sat there I was thinking of Charlie Robertson the Dunning stationmaster, who usually had only about fifteen or twenty passengers to contend with, suddenly being confronted by hundreds of children and none of them with tickets, which would undoubtedly upset him, since he was always adamant about collecting tickets.

I believe the big schoolroom was set out with rows of tables.

Prospective, adoptive parents, as you may say, came in and indicated what they would like: a single girl, a young girl, an older boy. Then the person at the table doing the allocating would say to me or the person from the other shed "Now go back and bring me a girl maybe six or seven years old" or "Are there a brother and sister available?" and I would go out to the shed. There were two teachers from Glasgow in each shed. And I would go out and tell them they're looking for a girl of a certain age, and the people have a grocery shop, or it's the doctor or the minister, or something like that.

To my recollection, the teachers made the selection. "I think this little boy would do for this one" and "I think this little girl would do for that one". And I would escort them into the school and take them to the table where the prospective parents were sitting with the allocator. The people in charge were all local, the worthies, you might say, the people of some establishment.

What surprised me at the time was how smoothly it all went. There was no trauma or hiccups or anything like that, it was just going constantly in and out with these requests for the children. And the other thing, I can recall few if any being sent back to the shed as being unsuitable for this particular person.

What I missed of course was what all the other villagers saw: the children coming up the street from the school, with their new parents. Apparently this was quite a sight. There was a continuous stream of prospective parents coming down and coming back an hour later with what they'd got. I missed all this because I was in the shed.

Amongst the waiting children there were a few tears but not a lot. The children sat there and played away. I can remember there was a bit of scrabbling about. They would take their gas mask boxes off. There were seats round the inside of the shed and they put the boxes on them. They had identification on them and some of them took the labels off and put them on the seat. I can remember the teachers getting a little bit annoyed at this. "Now you must always keep your labels on, you must keep your gas mask with you". "That's not your gas mask, that's mine. No, it's not"…and so on.

I think the allocating took about three or four hours, and we finished about seven o'clock at night. I don't know what happened to them when they came off the busses, perhaps they were fed in one of the other schoolrooms. There were never a lot of children in each shed, they came in about twenties and thirties, that was how many there were at any one time in the shed.

I struck up a good rapport with the teachers. They would say: "What's this Mr. and Mrs. So and So like, what do they do, are they nice, are they an elderly couple, are they a young couple?" And I would give them my impression of these people, knowing most of them, because the village wasn't as it is nowadays. The village was pretty static population wise. Everyone knew everyone else, and their reputations.

After an hour or so, one of the teachers said "Can we have a drink of water?" I said "Yes, I'll get water in the school".

There was a tap in the school and I got a couple of glasses. And I saw a look of consternation come over the face of one of the teachers. She lifted this glass up, and I think there had been a spate in the burn a few days before, because the water, which came from a water house on the burn above the village, looked a rather nice shade of sepia.

It wasn't just that. In it were floating, and perhaps even moving, all sorts of wildlife. And this teacher looked at this. "Do you drink that?" "Yes." I suppose to someone who had been used to fresh clear water from Loch Katrine coming out their mains taps, they'd never seen anything like this. I myself looked at the glass with surprise, seeing with new eyes the things moving in the brown water.

The impression I got was that she wouldn't even wash her feet in it, much less drink it. And that stuck with me, the look almost of horror on that young teacher's face.

I can remember in the sheds seeing the last one or two going over. Maybe they were getting a bit apprehensive that they weren't going to get anywhere. But they were all eventually allocated.

Afterwards, going up the street, I thought "Well, we've got two or three hundred new bodies in the village. Now these kids, they've been taken from their homes in the morning and here they are. They've going to have a strange pillow, they're going to be in strange surroundings, what are they going to dream about? They're going to wake up in the morning and they're going to see new streets, new shops, new people."

It would be interesting to hear what their reflections were, because I know I thought about them in these strange places, some on farms, some of them had never have seen a farm before. Some of them might have thought "This is great! This is a great adventure". But they were away from their folks, and they were going to wake up in the morning in a strange place. What sort of breakfast were they going to get compared to what they had before. Some of them might have a breakfast they'd never seen in their lives before.

***Jim Smith was born in Dunning in October, 1929,
and has lived all his life in the village:***

Jim Smith: I was nine when war broke out. The evacuees came in busloads from the station. I think everyone in the village was down to see them arrive because we'd never had an influx like that before. I suppose everyone was excited about it, what with the war starting. It was quite a dramatic period in the lives of the local people as well as the evacuees.

They were taken from their buses to the schoolyard, and then in groups from the schoolyard into the school. Then they were allocated to the families who were willing to take children in. We lived on Quarry Road in a one-level cottage but it had an inside toilet, which was quite unusual in the village at that time. We first got a family staying with us but I don't really remember them. Maybe it was because they got what we called the end room, with a separate door to the outside.

The main thing that I remember about the evacuees is that we went to school in the afternoon, and they went in the morning. This was at the big school in the village. It was only later on that the evacuees got separated into classes on their own up at the old cookery and woodwork classrooms. Also I remember we went to lift tatties in the morning, they went in the afternoon.

Two evacuees who came to us after about six months, John and Billy Laird, went to Middle Third farm at first, and their sister Bunty was separated from them. At one time she was in Kippen House. John was 13 when he came to the village, Billy was about nine and Bunty was in between. John also stayed a while at the manse with the Youngs.

The Lairds' mother came to visit them on Sunday, together with a lot of other parents, and I think about seventy five percent of the evacuees were back to Glasgow within two or three months. I think they just didn't like the village life. I suppose it was a wrench for them being away from their parents. It was a totally different life here from Glasgow, because you had really no entertainment, and in the evening it was all blacked out. You couldn't see a chink of light anywhere. They had got the blackouts up within a very short time.

Some things in the village at that time must have been a right shock to them. We still had a big percentage of dry toilets, and we also had the refuse collected by horse and cart. The only horses and carts these people might have seen may have been the brewery horses in Glasgow. Here the cart went round three times a week and collected the refuse and emptied the dry toilets. All the refuse including that from the dry toilets was collected at the same time, put in the cart, which had tin lids, and carted away.

Then, we still had no electricity at that time. We had a local gas works to produce gas for lighting, and the evacuees would have come from houses with electric light. We had a lot of coal fires. The same horse that pulled the refuse cart was used to pull the coal wagon.

There were also lots of farm carts about at that time, and in the Smiddy Close at the centre of the village was the smithy where the horses got shod. Anything up to five or six horses would be taken in the morning to get shod, and you could go down and see that happening. And you could also see rims being put on the cartwheels at the smithy. A lot of these things must have fascinated the evacuees.

There was a re-influx of evacuees when Clydebank got bombed, but it was never the same as that first arrival.

John and Billy Laird left after about two years to stay at Gask. I'm not sure why they left, but I think maybe it had become just too much for my mother to cope with, four or five growing lads and my father.

John became a good friend of mine, although not when he was staying with us. He came to Perth to do his National Service and he associated himself very much with Dunning and with us at that time. We became friends, and we visited back and forth as couples regularly. John died in 1994, just a short time after our first evacuees' reunion.

How did the evacuees get along with the locals? I don't think there was any animosity as such. When the big influx came they weren't really mixing much because it was dark nights, and that first autumn we were lifting tatties on the farms in the morning and they were there in the afternoon so there was no cross-mixing. It would only be when they were staying with somebody that they would mix. And as far as I could make out there was never any real problem with the people who took them in. There was the odd occasion when some of the people who got them weren't really wanting them and maybe weren't as nice to them as they could have been.

But the majority of cases…you know, a lot of them came back visiting for years after, so obviously they'd enjoyed their stay or they wouldn't have come back…it's a feature of the thing, if you dinna enjoy yourself you never go back.

Maybe the wrench was cushioned a bit for some evacuees. In the case of the Lairds it wasn't so bad because they had a brother with them. Also the majority came from the same school, so they had pals. It wasn't like me and others going away to the forces, you weren't with anyone local, you weren't with anyone you knew. I don't think I'd been ever been much out of the village at that time, because transport wasn't that great. The trains were there, right enough, but the farthest I ever got before I left for National Service was Stirling, a few miles away. We couldn't afford to travel. You were living in a very small community.

How did Dunning respond to the evacuees? Well, I think the country village responds to almost anything. It takes it in its stride.

You know, country people are adaptable. They dinna turn their nose up at anything, or get offended. Dunning people are very welcoming.

I always used to say when any stranger came to the village, we'll speak to you six or seven times. If you haven't answered by then, well then, on your bike. Being a villager myself of course I'm going to stick up for the place, but I feel it is a very friendly place. You feel the village is like a big family, and it just took in the new members of the family.

Dorothy Young, now of Blackford, Perthshire, was living at the manse of St. Paul's, the Dunning parish church, when war broke out.

Dorothy (Young) Benzies: I was the daughter of Peter Young who was the minister at St. Paul's Church, Dunning. My mother died two years before the war.

Rev. Peter
and Dorothy Young.

The first we heard about the evacuation was when my teacher, Margaret Johnston, arrived one evening with a folder. I happened to be there.

She was enquiring how many children we could accommodate in the house, and whether we would be prepared to take an adult. This was in the manse of St. Paul's church. We had five bedrooms. So the decision must have been to take one adult and two or three children.

I don't remember now how many children eventually turned up, two or three. And this little woman. She was small because I was quite tall for my age, and she was about my height.

But my goodness, we heard her all over the house. She didn't talk to the children, she screamed at them. I wasn't used to this, and I found this quite fascinating.

My father didn't find it quite so fascinating, especially on Fridays, which were quiet days. Fridays were sermon-writing days, and one had to be quiet. This made no difference to our little lady, who continued to scream at the children---who just ignored her. The more she screamed the more they ignored her.

I was at the big school. It seems a terrible thing to say now but one of the things about the war starting was that it was great fun because we got an extra week or fortnight off school. And the year the war started was the year I moved from the big school to Morrison's Academy in Crieff. So I don't remember anything of the evacuees in Dunning school.

All schoolchildren were issued with gas masks. They stayed in little square cardboard boxes, hung with a string around your neck. I was rather proud of mine and was very fussy about keeping it clean. I can remember when the evacuees arrived they can only have had their gas masks for a couple of days and their boxes were in a horrible mess. It's a silly thing to remember.

Our little lady had obviously never lived in the country before. Father was quite a keen gardener and grew the most magnificent vegetables. I remember to this day her going out with a great big bucket and absolutely pulling everything in sight, filling the bucket full of vegetables, coming in, chopping them up, and putting them in this enormous stew pan. She was given the use of the range in the kitchen, the housekeeper was given the cooker. Never the two would meet. And she would boil this up, and the range was covered with the remains of all the vegetables. Hysterically funny. The housekeeper, Mrs. Whitelaw, was very prim and proper. She was not amused. And father didn't want to know.

I do remember a slight problem of cleanliness with our first group of evacuees, especially with nits in the hair. I remember the housekeeper with her sleeves rolled up, and fine-tooth-combing the children's hair. Getting them bathed was another problem. I remember her saying "To the bath, to the bath". And they objected to being bathed, I don't know why, they just did.

Glasgow people are very warm-hearted, and I thought this little lady was very kind, and she was very good to me. I was a little bit frightened of her, but she was very kind to me. She was doing the best she could for her children, but the novelty of her screaming, and father saying "I will not tolerate this noise!" Especially on a Friday. It didn't seem to matter on the Sabbath, but on a Friday he would not tolerate it.

They didn't stay very long. There was this period of the phoney war, and gradually many of the evacuees returned to Glasgow.

Then we had another evacuee boy, John Laird. A very nice boy, rather quiet. After two or three months, we had another couple of boys, their parents were friends of my father's. One was Billy Gibb and the other was Ronny Stevenson. These boys both went to Morrison's Academy, and stayed with us about 18 months. By this time we were up to about 1944. Everything was quieting down. Most people had returned to Glasgow. They continued with us primarily I think to continue their education. I don't think it was awfully good for these children being chopped from one school to another. Their education did suffer quite a bit.

By this time my father had married again, so my stepmother had a lot of entertaining to do. We were a bit tight on certain foods: butter and eggs were available in the village, but when it came to meat it could be just a little bit difficult. My father had to have meat every day, he would not go for vegetarian food. So entertaining the boys' parents on weekends when they came to visit could be difficult.

The evacuation must have been a huge upheaval. To start with, it must have been a great adventure. But I think the novelty wore off very quickly, and that is why they went back so soon. They were completely out of their own environment, which is understandable. I mean, if I had been taken and thrown into the middle of Glasgow, I would have been completely out of my environment. I think you're very sensitive to environment as a child. Especially if you have a mother who screams at you all day long!

The fateful bus journey to Perth

Chapter 3: THE TEACHING EXPERIENCE

We hear now from three teachers from Haghill School in Glasgow who came to Dunning with the evacuees.

Mrs. Orma Burke (then Miss F.M. Orma Campbell), presently lives in Buderim, Queensland, Australia.

Mrs. Orma (Campbell) Burke: It is hard now to describe the feelings we all shared, pupils and teachers, as we were entrained immediately after the conclusion of Neville Chamberlain's speech, 11 am, September third, 1939. I remember standing in the train, looking out, and trying to guess where our destination might be!

Arriving in Dunning, this rather bewildered contingent was marched to the hall where billeting commenced. I vividly remember being given a hot <u>sweet</u> cup of tea.

I never did have sugar in tea, but that hot, sweet cup was delicious and probably was the best reviver for the state of near shock we were in.

It took time to billet the children. Then it was realised there was no accommodation arranged for teachers! "We" were three young women teachers from Haghill and one from a nearby Glasgow school. Someone suggested a small house in the High street. The owner was away, and after much anxious discussion a key was produced, along with permission to use half of the house, consisting of a bedroom upstairs, a bedsit downstairs, and a small kitchen. You can imagine how thankful we were to get anywhere to lay our weary heads. By now, it was dark. The house had no blackout curtains, so it was a struggle getting blankets to cover the windows. I remember the air-raid warden coming and saying to me: "We need it as black as that upstairs window, not a chink of light." I exclaimed: "But there is no light in that room!" He replied: "I know."

School was chaotic for a time, getting local and evacuee children sorted out together. We had to have morning and afternoon sessions to accommodate so many children. We used to run evening Games and Social Nights to try to relieve the kind people who opened their homes to evacuees. Everyone co-operated in a wonderful way.

I remember the autumn weather was glorious that year and people were so kind. I could have stayed on in Dunning with great pleasure, but duty called elsewhere. The first few months were termed 'the phoney war', as most people had imagined the war would start immediately. It did at sea, but the rest was ominously quiet. When nothing seemed to happen, it was a temptation for parents to take the children back home more than a desire on the children's part to return, as many had "never had it so good". By November '39, a majority of pupils had drifted back, so teachers were needed back in Glasgow. I returned to Haghill.

Miss Sydney Barr still lives in Glasgow.

Miss Sydney Barr: That Sunday morning, hearing the radio announcement of the Declaration as we waited with the children on the platform of Alexandra Parade station, was a dramatic moment which still comes back to me.

The long journey remains a blank but not the arrival in Dunning where a crowd of local people awaited us. After we were welcomed with food and tea the billeting began. I don't remember many tears, traumas or crises, perhaps because all members of families were boarded together. We teachers, three from Haghill and one from a senior school, were taken to "Sunnyside", a house on the main road which was unoccupied at the time. Life soon settled for pupils and teachers and we were accepted in the village. I remember the grocer telling us to go into his garden and pick his flowers as he had more than he would ever need. We were often invited out for an evening cup of tea and I wonder who it was who left the large basket of apples at our door when we had been seen going brambling.

Because of a death in the family I had to go back to Glasgow in early November. I have pleasant memories of the many kindnesses we received in the early months of war from the people of Dunning.

Mrs. Jenny Todd (formerly Miss Jenny Latto) was another member of the Haghill teaching staff who came to Dunning with the evacuees. She stayed longer than those we've just heard from, and the experience had a surprise ending. These memories were recorded in 1995, at her home in Dollar, Clackmannanshire:

Mrs. Jenny (Latto) Todd: I had lived with my mother in Pittenweem, on the Fife coast. I was born in the country there, so I've been a country person all my life. When I did start teaching I was in Wigtownshire, for five years. When I applied to Glasgow, I was given a post at Haghill, that was just two years before war broke out. So I really don't remember many of the children at all by name. But I was very fortunate because it was there that I met Mrs. Burke (Miss Orma Campbell) and Miss Barr, and I have kept in touch with them all these years.

The first thing I remember of our arrival in Dunning is that the children went in ones and twos into the school. We had to go with them and check their heads for nits. And take them off if they had any. I hadn't done that before. I knew there were such things because if you live in a rural area you had to be very careful yourself, and I had long hair in those days. We all had to start looking at our children's heads, to see if they were clean. And to our horror, many of them weren't. Horrified, because Denistoun, where Haghill School was located, was a very sort of decent middle class area at that time.

We teachers went into a rented house. We were very happy there, the four of us, Miss Campbell, Miss Barr, myself, and a teacher called Miss Mary Stark, from another school, possibly Whitehill.

Orma Campbell was the one who knew how to cook and do everything. One day she taught me to make a sweet of some kind, and it looked all right, very well indeed. But when we came to eat it we could not understand why it tasted of soap! It turned out there was a package of soap powder on the shelf, and someone had taken it down and sprinkled some of the contents on my sweet. So my efforts at cooking weren't a great success!

Miss Jenny Latto

One of my clearest memories is of 1940. At every break we went out and sat on a seat outside the school and the conversation was all about the evacuation from Dunkirk and the little ships going across the Channel. And such a beautiful June it was that year. All those boats going to rescue those poor men being shelled, we were getting it from the newspapers and it was constantly on our minds.

Teaching was difficult because we had to share rooms. Two classes had to share one room. It's not so easy teaching when in one ear you hear the voice of another teacher, and of course the children didn't like it.

That first autumn the other teachers went back to Glasgow, and I went into digs with a joiner. It was on the Auchterarder Road; he and his wife had their house, with his joinery right behind.

I was born myself in a wee village up from Pittenweem, called Newton of Balcomie, on December tenth, 1912. When my father died, it was a result of the First World War really, it was more a mental thing, I think. He died in 1922 when he was thirty-eight and I was ten. He had been in France, attending to broken telephone wires. What he had seen I think had disturbed him. He was all right apart from the fact that he used to have to get up, he couldn't sleep. He would go off for walks before work, and this day he didn't come back and they had to go looking for him. He had just sort of collapsed and his face had gone into the burn. And that was the end of that.

After a time the schoolmaster came to see my mother and said he hoped she could see her way to let me go on to the Wade Academy in Anstruther because I was just about ready for that. I was ten. My mother didn't get a pension. Widows' pension only started afterwards. She could have said you'll have to get a job, because we had to move out of the house. Fortunately I had an uncle and an aunt who were in a position to help and they took this house in Pittenweem and made some alterations to it and gave it to my mother.

I was the only child, and I never forgot what my mother let me do, go to the Academy and then to Dundee Training College for Teachers. I promised myself that I would teach for a number of years and reward my mother.

How did I meet my husband? Ah, that's another thing, and that makes Dunning very special.

Alan and I grew friendly at Dundee Training College. He had come over from St. Andrew's University to do his teacher training. They only had a short time there, the honour grads, to do their training. The matron was coming to the hall to meet this young man who had just arrived. I happened to be passing through the hall, and my first thought was, that's a good strong face that fellow has. That was all. Then we got to know each other. We were friendly when he was up in Dundee, and we kept in touch after.

Alan Todd

When I graduated in 1933 it was very difficult to get a teaching job in Fife because at that time there was a recession. The only girls who got in had fathers who were real levers and were in touch with some of the education committee. That was how it was done.

Three of us who really had better qualifications all had to go to the Borders. I felt I was going to the end of the world.

I had my mother down with me for a bit. If she had liked it I would have tried to get a little house. She didn't like it, it's an isolated place. But again the kindness of people…I'm still in touch with a family who had the little local shop.

But I was mindful of the promise I had made to myself that I would teach so many years and try to reward my mother. So eventually I wrote to Alan and said it wasn't fair to him and that we should cease to be friendly just now. That was in 1933. For six years we weren't in touch.

Every month out of the paltry salary I got…I remember it was ten pounds… I sent something to my mother and paid for digs and everything. Little did I know that she just stored it away and bought all my linen when I did get married!

After the Borders I moved to teach in at Haghill School in Glasgow, and I was there in 1939 when war broke out, and moved with the evacuees.

That's how it was when I came to Dunning. One day we went in by bus into Perth. A terrible journey when there were no lights on the bus. When we got to Perth I thought I saw a familiar figure. A little later, who should I meet on the street but Alan Todd.

From then on we didn't wait any more. I always remember the wife of the joiner where I was staying thought it was a bit much…the grapevine had worked and he was supposed to be friendly with someone in Auchterarder where he was now teaching. She thought…I don't know how to say it…I had snatched him away, but I explained that we were old friends. Anyhow, Alan and I decided we weren't waiting long. We married in Dunfermline in 1940 while I was still teaching in Dunning.

Wedding Day for Alan and Jenny Todd

It was just chance I bumped into him. And I must say now that my first impression couldn't have been truer. He was a wonderful person, Alan.

How many years had I vowed to work to repay my mother? I had in mind seven, and I did it. I did five in Wigtownshire and I was two years in Glasgow. So I did it. So I thought you're not lagging behind any longer. Oh, dear me!

I left Dunning in the summer of 1940 at the end of term. Alan had transferred from Auchterarder to Dollar Academy, and at Dollar we took charge of the boarding house for 12 years. He wound up Depute Rector.

How was it that neither of us had met anyone else in those six years? Well, if you met some of the male people where I taught, I can tell you, I would run a mile from them. It was well known that the teachers who came there finished up having to marry there. And so I thought, no way!

My husband had just been getting on with his life in Auchterarder. He taught there you see, and was friendly with someone, a cousin, on a farm there, I don't know her at all. That was what that Dunning landlady of mine was shocked at. She'd heard this and like all small places the news flies around, whether it's correct or not. And I had to reassure her that my husband-to-be was someone I had known before and not just five minutes ago.

As for our meeting again, it was meant to be, as some people might say. And that's why I have a particular personal affection for Dunning.

Alan Todd retired from Dollar Academy and he and Mrs. Todd had a long retirement before he died. She herself died a couple of years after this interview was recorded.

Stevenson College Edinburgh
Bankhead Ave EDIN EH11 4DE

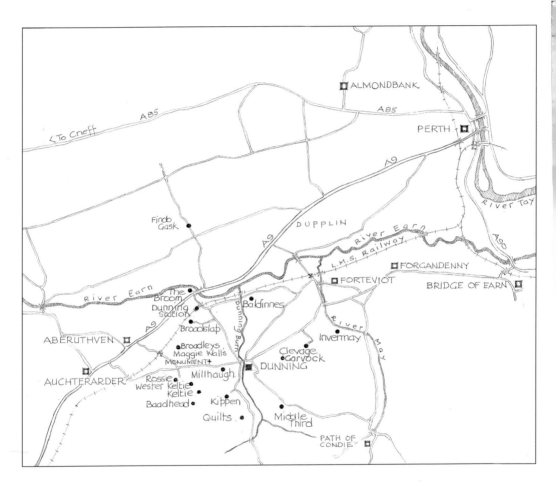

The area around Dunning

Short Stays

Chapter 4: ONE SISTER LEFT, ONE REMAINED

*Of the first influx of nearly three hundred evacuees who arrived in Dunning
on September 3, 1939, most returned to Glasgow within a few weeks or months.
Margaret Johnston came with her older sister Sheila.
Margaret left early, but Sheila stayed. Here are their stories:*

Margaret Johnston (now Mrs. Dick, of East Kilbride): My name was Margaret
Johnston. I was born March 22, 1934.

By the time war started, I hadn't really started school. My sister was three years
older than me, she was eight, then there was a gap of nine years to my older brother
and sister. The two oldest were working of course, so they weren't involved in being
evacuated.

When we were going for the train to come here, we all had to have our gas masks.
For some reason or other, I was being very thrawn. I refused to carry my gas mask.
There was no way I was going to carry that, I remember that clearly. Somebody else
had to carry it.

Being so young, I don't think I realised what was happening, that I was leaving
home, that I was going away from my mum and my dad. Later on, once I was here,
of course it hit me.

I created quite a bit of grief, I think. I used to sit looking out the window crying in
the house where we were. We lived with a couple whose name was Langstaff.

I was sitting by the window, wanting to go home, wanting to see my mummy. It was
dreadful. I don't think I stayed very long, just months actually. Because when my
mum and dad came to visit us, it would set me off each time to see them go away
again. I was just very much a mum's girl.

Sheila still has a postcard that she sent to my mum and dad. She wrote it in pencil
and one of the bits when she was finishing it up "and Margaret has been a good
girl". (laughs) I was the youngest, you see, so I think I was pretty much spoiled.

What do I think of the idea of the evacuation, of taking children away like that?
Well, obviously for me it was traumatic. Taking kids and putting them into a
completely strange environment, not knowing any people or the place where you're
going to or anything, I think it was heavy going for a youngster. And I would
imagine it would be tough on the parents too.

I don't know how it came about that I went back. It may have been that Mrs. Langstaff complained or wrote to my mother. Anyway the reason given was that she had become pregnant and couldn't look after us anymore. My mother came and took me away. She left my sister Sheila, because she was quite happy, she didn't mind. But I <u>had</u> to go home.

Sheila Johnston (now Mrs. Cope, of Glasgow): I remember leaving Glasgow, I had to carry two gas masks because my sister refused to carry hers. Mr. & Mrs. Langstaff were a very nice couple, maybe in their late twenties, early thirties.

He was a maths master at Strathallan School. We were there for the few months that Margaret was evacuated. The house was near the bridge facing the Kirkstyle Inn. The downstairs of the house was empty: I think it was a workman's place where they kept wood or tools.

We lived in the upper part. One thing I remember was that he taught me how to light the fire, showing me how to put the paper, the sticks and then the coals. I did that for them on a Sunday morning. I think they had a long lie-in, and I used to light the fire and make them a cup of tea.

When Margaret went away, I was moved to Kippen House, Lady Wilson's big house on an estate above Dunning. The ballroom was our bedroom. The housekeeper had her bed at the end where the band would have been, and we were at the top of the ballroom, four beds, four girls

There was a school up the Dragon, Newton of Pitcairns, and we went there. We had a mile and a half to walk, and then a mile and half back, every day, up to the big house. We didn't go up the main driveway, we went up the service road and in the servants' door.

Off the ballroom there was a sort of corridor, but it was big enough to be our sitting room. There was a small kitchen and a bathroom. In the corridor there was a big wooden panel (probably temporary), with a hatch in it. The maid would put our meals through this: silver salvers, silver lids, beautiful. I had a great war. I had wonderful food, partridge, I lived on the fat of the land up there, you know (laughs).

Lady Wilson always wore black, whether from being a widow or whether that was just her style. She was a very elderly lady. It was funny, when Lady Wilson's car used to pass, we all used to curtsy. Just the car passing, we'd curtsy whether she was in it or not.

We saw her in the grounds occasionally. We had the housekeeper, Mrs. MacPherson, who looked after us, employed probably by Glasgow Corporation, as the teachers were.

I don't really remember any bad times, except being lonely for my family. I think I was quite lucky, the age I was. I was born on the first of January, 1931. And I was lucky with the girls I was with. The four girls who were at Kippen when I was there were myself, Bunty Laird, Betty Neilson and Margaret Cruikshanks.

At Kippen House with housekeeper Mrs. Macpherson, L. To R.: Sheila Johnston, Betty Neilson, Martha 'Bunty' Laird, Margaret Cruickshanks

The other girls were about two years older than myself, I was the youngest. They were all nice to me.

There must have been an army camp not very far away, because this chap I remember was a dispatch rider. We would hear a dispatch rider in the distance and we'd say "I wonder if this is Thumbs Up." Because he used to come around the corner on his motorbike and whenever he saw us he used to take his hands off his bike and he went thumbs up like that, you see. So we were always desperate to know if this was Thumbs Up coming round on his bike.

The snow was wonderful, the cleanest I've ever seen. In the city the snow gets slush in no time, but here it was beautiful. Lady Wilson's daughter---she was called Lady May---she would get the chauffeur Jones to get this big toboggan she had. It could take the four of us. We played for hours on this thing, and coming down through the hills was beautiful.

The exciting bit was always when the bus came on a Sunday, bringing the parents to visit. By this time my brother was in the R.A.F. and I remember him coming one time in his uniform and I thought this was just wonderful. It must have taken a lot of time to come from Glasgow because in these days there were no motorways. They didn't come by train. I think the parents just got together and hired a bus at a pound a head or maybe ten shillings. It wouldn't have been very much and the bus was always full.

I must have been here about a year and a half to two years. From Kippen I went off to a friend of my aunt's near Dunoon. But they were bombing Greenock at this time, and we were nearer the bombing in Dunoon than had we been in Glasgow. So from there we went to Bannockburn, to another friend of my aunt's. We came home from there when air raids had pretty well stopped in Glasgow.

I've been back to Dunning a few times. The first time we drove up to Kippen it was a private house and we just drove out again. We came another time and we learned in the village it was getting renovated. So we went up and I said to the workmen would it be all right to go in and see it, and we got in to see the ballroom. I was able to say "that's where my bed was" and it was lovely to see it again.

Billeting headquarters: Dunning Primary (The 'Big School')

Chapter 5: THE FINAL STRAW

The three youngest of the Cassidy family were evacuated to Dunning. Only the two girls, Margaret and Isobel, have any recollection of the experience (their young brother remembers nothing). The two sisters had totally different reactions to being evacuated, one disliking it, one loving it.

Older sister Margaret (now Mrs. Little, of Bishopbriggs): My stay in Dunning was brief and my memories are not particularly happy.

At eleven years old I was very excited to hear the intimation on the wireless about the intended evacuation. My mother even got the applications for evacuation to Canada, but she stopped short at filling them in.

There were four youngsters in our family, and our father had been dead for five years. My elder brother was fifteen, and he had no intention of being evacuated. Before the war was over, he was seriously wounded at Monte Cassino in Italy. I was eleven, and my sister was eight, nearly nine. My younger brother was five.

I remember lots of people waiting at Dunning School, which seemed to be too small to be a school after the size of Haghill. There were lots of men with lists, and the evacuees were allocated very speedily. Most people, I seem to remember, wanted two of the same sex. That was understandable if they only had one spare bed. Some were more specific about the age, and sometimes one kid was pulled from one group and placed in another without any explanation.

Quite soon nearly all the children were gone, and we three Cassidys were still there. This was partly because I was a big girl, my growth spurt came early and I was the same size at ten as I am now. And I was strictly obeying my mother's specific instructions: we were not to be separated.

So I was clutching my wee brother's hand every time somebody tried to remove him, attractive little fair-haired boy as he was.

In the end, we were put in a car…that was a big excitement for us…with one other ten year old girl from our street, Myra Campbell. And we were driven to a billet where the owners had decided not to turn up and collect their enforced allocation of four evacuees.

And thus we entered the Old Parsonage, Dunning. By the front door, for the first, and only, time.

It seemed like a mansion to me. But seeing it forty years later I saw it was just a modest, substantial country house. The lady of the house and her two daughters, probably in their thirties, were not at all pleased to see us. There was another altercation about our being a mixed-sex group. Anyway, it was decided that because we were three of a family, and the boy was young, we would have to stay. We then passed through into the servants' quarters, into the charge of Charlotte the cook and Honour the parlor maid, and thence into a big room near the kitchen which was empty except for a chest of drawers.

Later that night, some men delivered two palliasses and these straw sacks on the floor were our beds for all the time we stayed there.

Three elegant ladies, in their long evening gowns, briefly looked at us before going in to dinner, after hearing the gong ringing. Poor Charlotte and Honour had had to attend to getting us to bed before serving their mistresses dinner. Charlotte, or Lottie as we called her, advised us that if the lady of the house or her daughters spoke to us, we should bob and add "Ma'am" to our reply. And though my socialist hackles rise at this now, I quite enjoyed it at the time.

What a mystery we must have been to them. I don't know whether Dunning people realised that East End evacuees weren't all of one category. We in the East End, even as young as seven, eight, nine could classify ourselves.

There were three schools there. There was Bluevale, Haghill, and there was Alexandra Parade. Two hundred yards at the most separated them. But we were aware that the people from Bluevale were slum clearance children. These were the type of youngsters who have gone on the record as the typical Glasgow evacuee. In Haghill, we were the middle category, a mix of council housing, not quite the best, not slum clearance. Most of us who came from this intermediate housing had originally come from over-crowded private letting, some with just a lavatory, most with no bathrooms. Nevertheless, our parents felt they were coming down in the world going into council housing. We attached much more significance to the Alexandra Parade children, who lived in the more substantial private letting, red sandstone with the wally (tiled) close which is a very meaningful expression. That was everybody's ambition, to move to a property with a wally close. Council property was never built that way.

The point I'm making is that all evacuees were not germ-ridden, poverty-stricken, illiterate, unused to comfort, as the picture has been painted of them, particularly those from the East End of Glasgow.

After about three weeks my mother came to visit. A coach had been organised by the neighbours. My mother was most unhappy to find us lying on straw mattresses or bags of straw. She was told at the school that our host family had been offered beds and had refused them. Now I don't know what the explanation was. Maybe, now that I'm sensible, fresh straw was fresher than a soiled mattress from an ex-army disposal, I don't know. Anyway, that really annoyed her.

This is the bit where I'm really going to curl up with embarrassment. The ladies of the house said we had nits in our hair. Now at eleven years old, when puberty's just beginning, the embarrassment...I've no recollection of nits being identified before I came to Dunning, but I'm sensible enough now to realise it's possible we could have had nits.

My mother was a widow for all those years. Before the war there was no way for a woman to earn money. Her pension at that time added up to twenty-four shillings a week. Ten shillings for herself, which is fifty pence by today's money. Five shillings, which is twenty-five pence, for the oldest child and three shillings for each of the three other children: that's the total amount which she was allowed. My mother's only source of extra income was to take in lodgers. At the time war broke out we had two girl lodgers, one of whom, Cathy, got her hair done about every second week. It was a tight marcel wave, and it was never disturbed, never washed, until the next time. Now Cathy and I were great friends, so quite possibly I did have nits.

Anyway, our host family said we did, so our hair was shorn. It wasn't shaved, but it was cut exceedingly short, and treated with a smelly ointment. Sixty years later, I still curl up with the embarrassment of having to turn up at school with that hair cut. They talk today about selective memory…my sister recollects that we in fact we did stay away from the school next day…I don't recall that, because I was a very law-abiding, obedient girl.

The Cassidys Of Denistoun, Glasgow, pre-War: L. To R. Margaret, Isobel, James, John

Younger sister Isobel Cassidy (now Mrs. Bernard of Denistoun): Being that wee bit younger than Margaret I didn't have the sensitivity that she had about this hair-cutting and things. I do remember the time we 'plunked' (skipped) the school and being asked "Where were you today?" We replied "At school." Unknown to us, the headmaster had phoned and reported that we weren't at school. So then the three girls, Margaret, Myra Campbell and myself had to sit down and write so many times on paper "I must not tell lies". My brother, who was too young to write, had to stand with his face in the corner for a certain time as punishment.

To me I felt the family were the Queen and Princesses. I knew they were superior. I was probably too young and too stupid to realise they were looking down at us. I realise now they were condescending, but I thought then that that was how people of that standing behaved.

Older sister Margaret: Another thing happened when my mother came on that first visit. She got on the coach to go back. The other neighbours were showing off money that their children had made at the potato picking. All of us had gone along and picked potatoes. But where the Pickens and the Lothians and the Lairds had money for their mothers, we didn't have any. If there was money going my mother could certainly have done with it as well as anyone else. So next time she came back, she made enquiries about where our potato money had gone, and the farmer said that the our host family had said not to give us any money but rather to send a bag of potatoes to their house.

Again it seems a sensible thing. We were getting fed. But the money that would have come from this potato picking would have been such a major factor in our lives. And my mother was further enraged that we were still on the straw six weeks later. She'd been told that first visit that beds were coming, but instead of beds there was a further delivery of straw.

My mother was a very forthright and not ready-to-be-put-upon lady and believed that her children were as good as the next one's. She wasn't at all pleased with the ladies' inference and condescension. She pulled a sheet from the top of the palliasses, put everything we possessed in it, tied a knot in it, and pulled us away on to the coach and home.

Younger sister Isobel: I can remember getting off the bus on the trip home from Dunning. The bus-driver—it was dark, it was the blackout, that would be three children, my mother, getting off the bus with this big sheet tied in the middle with all the belongings that we had—I can remember the bus-driver saying, to the rest of the passengers in the bus, "Stand back, the war's finished." And we all bundled off. It was a family saying for years after that, something we laughed about.

The experience didn't put me off wanting to go back to another evacuation. After I'd been home for a year or so, the bombs were falling. When the siren went, everybody went down to the ground flat of the house and huddled in the hallway. Thinking about it now, if the house fell in, it'd fall and hit you.

The second time I was evacuated my young brother came with me. Margaret didn't go, that was her finished with evacuation. Jim and I went to a place called Canonbie in Dumfries-shire. Again it was the same situation. You were lined up in the school playground, allocated to a family. Some of the girls I knew landed in luxury, with horse-riding facilities and a beautiful bedroom to themselves and everything. Jim and I landed with a farm labourer. The man was an alcoholic but we didn't realise that at the time, we were too young. It was homely, just a poor house. An outside toilet, we weren't used to that. I was there for ten months and got treated there just like the family. There was a son just a bit older than me and a girl the same age as my brother. I think she was doing it for the money because they'd be paid to take us. But we got taken to the auntie's house and the granny's house just like her own children were.

I can remember on that evacuation, too, being sent to the village on my cycle and there was a big steep hill outside the cottage. I had to take the accumulator, which charged up the wireless sets in those days, and it would be full of acid. There was a glass box and I had to put that over the handlebars and shoot down the hill. I was only about eleven at the time, and when you think of the danger of it now, whew!

After about ten months my older brother was being sent overseas with the army. My mother decided the whole family would visit my brother in Aberdeen barracks before he left. When we got home there was a letter on the mat from my host mother to say that while we had been home she and the little girl had been on the way to visit the grandma and the bus carrying them had been in an accident with an army lorry crossing the river Esk. The wee girl had been killed, and the mother had had an arm torn from the socket. We would have been on that bus going to Granny's as well. We were never back after that.

Then, after I can't remember how long, I got itchy feet again. The war was still on and I wanted to go again. My chums were going. This time it was like a holiday camp place. It was called Glengoner camp in Abingdon, in Lanarkshire and included children from all over Glasgow, not just East End children. Some of them were pretty tough and it was a case of survival of the fittest. If you laid something down and it wasn't chained on to you it would go missing. I had been sent away with a new coat and hat and all the rest of it! Mother came down after about ten days. I was fading away with the conditions there so she whipped me home again. I was only myself that time, no brother or sister. That was ten days, ten months the previous time, and six weeks in Dunning.

Chapter 6: AND SO WE WENT HOME

Most of the nearly 300 evacuees to have come to Dunning in the first influx didn't stay very long. Here are a few recollections which explain why. First Sheila Cameron (now Mrs. Long of Auchterarder, Perthshire):

Sheila Cameron, Hilda MacMillan

Sheila (Cameron) Long: I was born and brought up in Dundee, where I started school in 1938. At the outbreak of war, the schools in Dundee were closed for security measures and evacuations were planned for all the children. My parents made a private arrangement for me to go to Dunning with a young friend of mine, Hilda McMillan, who was also six. Mother had a maiden aunt who lived in Dunning.

We were enrolled at the local primary school, and taken up the hill to the little infant school which we discovered was very crowded indeed with Glasgow evacuees. There were so many that they had to have morning school and afternoon school.

My main memory of that infant school is that the teacher was tremendously harassed. She had quite an unruly bunch of children, though we were only five and six years old.

A child behind me had broken up a piece of chalk, and from the back of the room was throwing pieces at my head. I suffered it for so long while the teacher was writing on the blackboard. Finally I snapped and picked up a piece of this chalk, turned round and threw it. And of course guess who was caught? That was my very first taste of corporal punishment and the tawse. No mercy, no explanations, just come up and hold out your hand. Whack! So I was most upset. In Dundee, where I'd come from there was really never anything like that. There was never any problem of indiscipline in school.

I think I must have spent about a week in that school, perhaps more. It was decided that all six year olds would be transferred down to the big school, as we called it.

Our new classroom was very bare, tremendously crowded, desks in rows, looking at the teacher who seemed to be sitting on a very high stool, at a very high desk. She seemed to tower over us. I don't remember much about the lessons that first day, but the day that does stick in my mind was when, at the end of the afternoon, she read out a list of names. These children were to stay behind after school. So I said to this local girl who was sitting by me, "Why do we have to stay behind?" And she said "Well, if you get more than five mistakes in spelling, you stay behind and get the belt."

My friend Hilda's name was also read out and I whispered to her "Are you going to stay behind to get the belt?" "No, are you?" "No, I'm certainly not. Let's go." So while the teacher had a group around her desk, we crept down as near to the floor as we could reach, practically on all fours, crept past her, made a lightning dash down the corridor, out the door, down the path, home to the old lady, and said "We're never, ever going back to that awful school again!"

The old lady then had the problem of entertaining two small children, and I don't think she really understood what she had let herself in for. She arranged that a pile of sand be brought into the garden and proceeded to buy us one spade and one bucket, and expected us to share. Well of course two six year olds, one wants the spade when the other wants it, and we ended up fighting really quite badly, and hitting one another over the head with this spade.

Finally the old lady just gave up on us, and asked our parents to take us home.

When we arrived home, the schools were still closed. We had home school, in the house. Looking back, I think evacuating from Dundee was perhaps a bit premature. There really wasn't much bombing in Dundee. In total I think 3 or 4 bombs. I think they over-reacted in closing the schools.

Wilda Berkeley (now Mrs. Olley of Hepplestow, North Lincolnshire) spent considerably longer in Dunning.

Wilda (Berkeley) Olley: I was evacuated to Dunning in 1939. I was nine years old. I think I was here for about 18 months, I can't quite remember. We went to the billeting place in Dunning and all these foster parents were gathered there. They said "Two girls" and I grabbed this girl whom I knew from school, Myra Anderson, she wasn't a friend but a girl I knew, and we went forward and we were billeted with Mr. & Mrs. John Glenn of Wester Clevage farm. He was the farm hand there.

Wilda Berkeley

We were happy there. They were very good to us. I had come from a tenement in Glasgow. It had all mod cons, but it was a tenement. The cottage here, that the farm hand had, had no electricity, and the loo was a bucket at the end of the garden, in a little shed at the bottom of the garden. You just accept all these things really, and we were quite happy.

The Glenns were quite young. They had a little boy, about twelve months to two years, also called John.

We went to the village school. I remember when we came out of the school door, we could look down at the village and see the church with the clock. I recall this because once the teacher asked me to go out and tell her what time it was on the church clock. I got out there, and I thought "Well, I can't really tell the time" but I didn't want to admit that. So I stood there for a bit, and then somebody came along and I said "Could you tell me the time please, because I can't quite see the clock from here?" I was a bit devious, wasn't I?

I didn't feel particularly homesick. The farmhand and his wife made me feel at home. John Glenn, my foster father, made a little trolley and he used to run round with us on the back of it, round and round the house. And he had a nice garden. He used to take us out into the countryside. I call him my foster father because that's what he was really. They were a nice couple, and it was good of them to open up their house for us. He was tall, broad, and I suppose quite handsome, though I wasn't thinking much about that in those days. I think they would be in their thirties.

I seemed to fit in well with the life. I was adaptable.

The other girl didn't stay as long as I did. Because she didn't write home, her mother came down one day to visit her, and she was in a really foul mood. She shouted at Myra, saying "So many weeks, and never a letter!" So she took her home with her. She just took her home. A bit silly really.

So I was left on my own then, for a bit. I think the lady thought I was homesick, because I was quieter, having lost my friend. Not doing the usual things we had done before, but I was quite happy really. But she took me aside one day and said "I've written this to your mother, and she's going to think you're homesick," she said, "but I won't post it unless you want me to." Of course when she started talking like that I started to cry, although I'd felt quite happy. She said "Shall I post the letter? " and blubbering, I said "Yes." But as I say, I was really very happy, though I went back then to Glasgow.

Wilda (Berkeley) Olley on a return trip to Dunning, 1998

Alice Beveridge (now Mrs. Donaldson of Glasgow) was almost six when she and her two bigger sisters came to Dunning from Haghill School. Their stay was the brief one typical of the majority of the first evacuees.

Alice (Beveridge) Donaldson: We weren't here too long. I was with my sisters. Cathy, she's 18 months older than me, and my sister Eleanor would be about 3 years older than me.

We went to stay with Miss Monteith. It's up a hill in the village somewhere. It was very nice at Miss Monteith's. It was a lovely big house, and she was very good to us. But I wanted home. I think I was too young to be away from my mother, because we had a good life.

I just came running down the hill one time, with my label round my neck, crying.

44

We didn't wear them all the time, but I had just put it round my neck, wanting to go away. My mother had come over that Sunday with a mamma doll in her bag. She had come on the bus and was walking up the hill, and I was running down the hill to meet her. And I just said I wanted to go home.

When I started crying, my oldest sister started to cry. She wanted to go home as well. That was Eleanor. Then the one in between, Cathy, she started crying too. She wanted to stay.

So Miss Monteith said she was sorry, Mrs. Beveridge, she couldn't afford to keep the house open for just one girl

And that was it, we all went home. That would be I'd say six months after we arrived here.

I can't remember anything at all about the school. I just wasn't happy at all. I was happy enough in the house we were staying, and Miss Monteith was very good to us, she couldn't have been any better. We always had an apple and a cup of milk before we went to bed. And she would sit and cut out pictures for us, and make paper dolls, you know. She was really excellent.

We were back in time for the air raids. But my mother never tried to evacuate us anywhere else, she just kept us there. I remember getting up and going to Alexandra Park to the shelters when there were air raids on.

Three members of the Picken family arrived together in Dunning, five year old Malcolm, seven year old Ian and almost eleven year old Margaret. Margaret and Malcolm tell us about it.

Margaret (Picken) Black: I remember after arriving in Dunning waiting to be "billeted" and becoming increasingly anxious as I realised that most of the children had been claimed and feeling that perhaps we were unwanted.

Eventually my two brothers and I were on our own along with another family of three children, the Lothians, who lived near us at home. And then to my immense relief we were all dispatched to the Manse with the Rev. and Mrs. McKinnon.

As we were three girls and three boys I expect it was not too difficult to accommodate us, although I did feel the boys had a much larger room than the girls!

It was quite a shock to find that we had to sleep on straw mattresses on the floor. I'm afraid I failed to think of this as an adventure and I shed a few tears before falling asleep. I'm glad to stay it wasn't long until we all had our own beds.

St. Serf's Manse in Dunning

Our rooms were near the top of the house and I loved to walk round the boys' room (the "nursery" I remember it was called). The boys' room was definitely more interesting than the girls'. Along one wall underneath the windows were low cupboards and we soon discovered it was possible to crawl through the cupboards without having to go in and out of the doors. Great fun! There was also a large walk-in cupboard which had loads of magazines and journals stored there, including Punch.

The eldest of the other three children, Margaret Lothian, was a girl on ages with myself. Each Saturday afternoon, Mrs. McKinnon gave lessons in First Aid to ladies from the village, and both of us were used as models for the bandaging sessions. I felt very important on these occasions and was so pleased when I learned how to roll bandages correctly.

However, the wonderful thing for me about these Saturdays was that the whole atmosphere of the nursery, which was used for the purpose of the First Aid, was completely changed. There was a fireplace at one end of the long room and there was always a huge fire burning on those days with nursery posters on the walls, and I'm sure that afternoon tea was served. When all the ladies had gone home and I had successfully rolled the bandages, I loved to fetch the Punch magazines from the cupboard, and I would sit on the floor in front of the fire and pore over them until the fire eventually died down. I don't know where the boys were at this time— keeping well out of the way, I expect!

As both us older girls were named Margaret, it was decided by Mrs. McKinnon that I would be called Rita, to avoid confusion. I must say I wasn't impressed by that name!

It was marvellous having fields to romp in, being enthralled by the rabbits and other animal life, and finding fruit trees to raid (naughty!).

I well remember another family of three children who had been neighbours at home and who were billeted in a large house called the "Parsonage". One of them, Isobel, just a year or two my junior, was often corrected in her speech. For example, if she said she was sweating she was told she was perspiring. Well, one afternoon we had had a wonderful time romping around and had great fun throwing "itchy coos" or burrs at each other. They were sticking all over our jumpers. When our friends went home for tea and were asked what they had been doing, Isobel, not wishing to be corrected yet again, said we had been gathering itchy COWS! At that age we thought this was hilarious.

I had my eleventh birthday at the end of October and my mother sent a birthday cake and a new pair of wellies so that I could wade in the burn with the others. What heaven!

The driveway of the Manse facing the Thorn Tree was lined with elderberry trees, and the berries were used to make the communion wine for the Church. I remember the large Communion Cup being passed around. At home in Glasgow our Church had small individual glasses. Harvest Thanksgiving also has a place in my memory. We all took a small bunch of sweet peas from the garden. At home, I would have had something like a large cabbage, and at that age I couldn't help making a comparison.

Although my few months' stay in Dunning was short in comparison with that of some other evacuees, it has always represented a very special time. I must also have been homesick. We were visited by my Mother or Father, and one Sunday when my Father arrived I suddenly burst into tears and had great difficulty in trying to explain what was wrong. My Father must have been upset, and after questioning me, made the decision to take the three of us home and he packed our things together.

Malcolm Picken: Life was good for us here, but it was very rough to try to come to terms with the fact that our parents weren't with us. My father of course was working at that time and my mother had my brother, who was only a year old, he was too young to have come to an evacuation.

I was just five and a half, but I can still remember a few things that happened. Lord Rollo's gamekeepers kept the manse supplied with meat like rabbits and other wild meat. One morning the teacher asked what we had all eaten the night before, and trying to impress, I raised my hand and said "I had wooden pigeon" for a meal, instead of wood pigeon. Of course the whole classroom was in an uproar, and I couldn't understand why they were laughing.

But most memorable was just being able to play around by the burn by the bridge. Many a night when I came back to the manse, I was scolded because I was soaking wet. We'd gone into the river to fish, just with a piece of string and a stick and a bent hook. I could spend hours there.

Another place to visit was the blacksmith's shop, where we used to rummage and collect the old horseshoe nails. The blacksmith was a very kind soul. One night he went away and locked the door and he didn't know we were still inside. There were two of us there, me and another young chap. My brother discovered I was missing and he knew I'd been at the blacksmith's shop. He came down and heard us banging on the shop door and had to go and get the blacksmith to open up.

I remember at that time the young men, the late teen-agers, were being conscripted into the army and being sent away for training for this big war that was going to take place. And of course their girlfriends were eager that they would make a commitment. The minister spent a lot of Saturday mornings marrying the couples in the hallway of the Manse. For expediency, before the boyfriends went away to the army. Many of them didn't come back. We used to be able to sit at the top of the stairs, lean over the banister and look down into the hall and watch the minister with the marriage ceremony.

All too soon, my father had missed us so much that he came up at one stage and took us home. The period of time here must have been three to four months only, and we never ever came back again.

Footnote: Years later, when Malcolm Picken and his future wife, Aline Simpson, were courting, they were surpised to discover that they had been evacuees in almost adjacent Perthshire villages. Aline had gone with a party of evacuees on Sept 1/39 to Forgandenny. She appears at the very bottom of the photograph on the right, which also is featured on the cover of this book. The photograph was taken by A.C. Cowper of Perth, and is reprinted in this book with the kind permission of the copyright holders, Louis Flood, photographers, Perth.

Betty Robertson became Mrs. Lucien Laing. She came to the Dunning evacuee reunions of 1994 and 1995, and died on Boxing Day, 1995. She wrote this reminiscence after the first reunion.

Mrs. Betty (Robertson) Laing: On evacuation day, my sister Jean (now deceased) and I were taken by my mother down to Haghill School. My sister was 13, I was 11. My mother had made a picnic for us, which I had finished before we left Glasgow.

When we got to Dunning, Jean and I were billeted with a Miss Marshall in Laggan House, where we were made very welcome by her and given some milk and biscuits.

We wrote a note to my mother to tell where we were staying and on our return to the house Miss Marshall told us one of our teachers would also be staying with her. She had difficulty in remembering the name of the teacher. Jean and I named a few whom she did not know. We then suggested one more name and discovered that the teacher was one known as Haggie Bags: and we experienced some dread. My sister had a rash on both cheeks which was harmless but Haggie Bags made my sister's life a complete misery. She would not allow anyone to sit beside her or share a book with her. At almost every meal she asked if we appreciated what a lovely clean house we were living in and I wondered what kind of house she thought we came from.

We were in the garden one day with another two children from Haghill School shelling peas for Miss Marshall, when Haggie came round and asked Jean if she should be shelling them when we all had to eat them, whereupon Jean burst into tears.

Left: Jean and Betty Robertson

Next day in class Jean was in a terrible state and when we came out of school we went to the square where there was a telephone box, whereupon I telephoned my mother at her work and told her what was happening to Jean, while a lot of Glasgow kids were round the box shouting for me to tell my mother what was said and done. Next day my mother arrived in Dunning to take us home, but the headmaster pleaded with her to let us stay. My mother said we were not staying another night in the same house as Haggie.

We were taken out to Garvock Estate to stay with the gardener and his wife, a Mr. & Mrs. McArthur who were great. I enjoyed my time at Garvock but I am afraid Jean hated it. We went tattie picking and thought we were rich with wages. It was hard work but I loved it and we came home on the horses. Unfortunately Mr. McArthur was retiring and as the house was a tied house we had to move back into the village.

We went to live with the baker at Robertson's shop. We were there for a while but again Jean was not happy at all. One day she decided she wanted to go home. We packed our bags and made our way to Belle Flockhart's shop. She kindly had her son drive us down to the station. We arrived home to find my mother had the door all locked up and was very surprised to see us.

Lasting Impressions

Chapter 7: HIDE, IT'S THE GERMANS!

For some people, the war and the evacuation gave the chance of a fresh start.
That was the case for the Forbes family. Four of the five children who came to
Dunning with their widowed mother tell us about it.

Jemima Forbes (now Mrs. Townsley of Darvel, Ayrshire): My father had died in 1937. He worked for the Singers factory in Clydebank. My mother was left with five children. I was born December tenth, 1929. I'm the third oldest, I have two older brothers and a younger brother and a younger sister.

When the war was about to start in 1939 my mother had heard about being evacuated and she decided we would go. She thought maybe it would be a new life. She couldn't go out to work after my father died because she was so busy looking after the five of us.

Before we knew it we were in the train coming to Dunning. That's really the biggest thing I remember in my life, leaving the station at Alexandra Parade, and being in the carriage and the schoolteacher with us. I remember I heard the newspaperman shouting "War declared! War declared!" And I heard the teacher say to my mum "We'll not discuss it in front of the children", meaning what was going to happen.

I also remember all the families waiting for people to come to take them. My mother was with this other lady, Mrs. Macnab, who had three children. It was near the end before we and the Macnabs were shouted at to come. When we went outside there was a great big limousine waiting for us, because the chauffeur at Keltie Castle had come down to collect us in the car.

David Forbes, Cumbernauld: Though I was just six I remember quite a lot. It was exciting, coming from tenements to a country place. We stayed at first in Baadhead Cottage on the farm up behind Keltie Castle, at the foot of the Ochil Hills. It probably took me a year to get used to the big open spaces.

There were two cottages. I think they were servants' quarters for the Castle. The Macnabs shared a cottage with us. We'd come from a big housing scheme in Glasgow, and there, when you went out to play, there were twenty or thirty kids to play with. At Baadhead you felt at first lost and lonesome, just your family.

Jemima (Forbes) Townsley: When we arrived at the cottage, there was no electricity. We had to light candles. We had some food with us, including York chocolate, the dark chocolate you didn't like when you were young. I remember

Keltie Castle

in the cutlery drawer there were a lot of wooden spoons and you couldn't cut anything up. It was just different.

There were two ends to the house. I think it was a doctor's holiday house. The end my mother got was really beautiful. The end Mrs. Macnab got was the maids' end. My mother used to say "Well you're no playing in here, you'll play in Mrs. Macnab's end." We weren't allowed to touch anything in the bit we stayed in. And my two older brothers went over to a farmhouse to sleep.

There was water and there was a bathroom in the house, but no electricity. There were beautiful paraffin lamps to be lit. However, my mother was frightened to light them. She said "Oh better not light them in case any of you come up against them and break them or something". Instead we lit the candles. In fact Mr. Hogg the grocer used to say "What does ye dae up there, does ye eat the candles?" We were always down to him for candles.

We were always in Mrs. Macnab's end because we would just sleep at our end. My mother would cook with Mrs. Macnab and do different things at her end.

When we went down the road to school, once we got started, we went in the afternoon and the Dunning folk went in the morning. Then things changed. David and I went to that wee school up the road and Tommy and Willie went to Auchterarder High. David and I walked miles and miles to school.

David Forbes: It was a long way to go to school, I think three or four miles or more. It was cold in winter, but there was nothing you could do about it. You just accepted it. We walked down to the Auchterarder road past the Castle, where the family then was the Queen Mother's relations, the Bowes-Lyons. I remember the first Christmas, my mother and the others were worried about noises outside. All of a sudden a big knock comes at the door.

We're in this lonely cottage and suddenly this knock comes!

Jemima (Forbes) Townsley: My mother said "Oh my goodness, the Germans have come!" and we hid under the table. And here it was the people from the Castle, the Bowes-Lyons, with gifts for us…a big sack of gifts. They were Santa Claus that night. It was just a wonderful Christmas they gave us.

David Forbes: They gave us toys, and they gave my mother perfume. Probably my mother didn't know what perfume was at that time. They gave the other family the same things.

Jemima (Forbes) Townsley: The Bowes-Lyons had a boy John and he went to school but he was chauffeur-driven. We got friendly with him for a while, and then they let us come through the Castle grounds because it was a short cut for us. They were really good to us.

Then Mrs. Macnab became pregnant so she moved into the village. We moved into her end of the cottage, and two old maids came and lived in the end my mother had.

Jessie Forbes (now Mrs. Dale of Armadale, West Lothian): I was the youngest, born March thirteenth, 1935. I remember mostly what my mother told me of our stay in Dunning. The old maids next door, it was my birthday, and they gave me a wee chair and sweets and a cup, I can remember that. Or I can remember my mother telling me. I had that wee chair for years. I gave it away to my uncle to give to other poor children who had nothing.

I can just remember my grandfather coming up to visit us and he fell in the burn coming up to the house. My mother sent my brothers down to get him.

Jemima (Forbes) Townsley: We were here two years altogether. Then we moved into the village too. The winter had been so bad that my mother asked to get moved into Dunning.

David Forbes: We loved the summer months, which were beautiful. In winter, it was dark at four, the candles were lit and that was you in the house for the night, you couldn't do anything outside.

Then we moved down to the village. The bakery was next door, and I used to look out the window and watch the rats playing about.

An exciting thing was going to a farm near the village to watch the bats flying about at night under the light, hundreds of bats you could see floating about there. It was the entrance to a farm then, but I think now it's the entrance to the swing park.

I could never go anywhere unless I was with my two older brothers. Tommy had a milk run and I used to go with him in the morning, delivering milk. And we used to go berry-picking with my mother on the farms.

With hindsight, when you look back on it, it was a good experience, being an evacuee. I think it educated you a lot regarding country life. Although I was only six or seven, you got in the way of working the country style. When you see something on television about the country, you think, now that was the same in Dunning, and you remember the local folk and their ways.

Tommy Forbes, Erskine: At Baadhead we had a living room, kitchen, and a bathroom. There were six of us counting my mother so we were quite crowded. The cottage was right across the road from the farm where my brother and I slept.

The cottage was a good way up the estate. You passed by the castle, and the gardener's house. You had to open and close the gates as you went up. The last time we came we went and looked at the cottage. It's completely derelict now. And the gamekeeper's cottage, Willie McGinn's, it's completely away.

Whenever there was a pheasant shoot or a fox hunt, Willie McGinn used to get us to go to it. I think we got about five shillings and a meal at the Castle. We sat with all the gamekeepers, and the lords and ladies sat in another room.

Lady Wilson lived on one of the roads up from the village, and when she had a shoot at her place, Willie McGinn used to take my brother and me there too. We were beaters, chasing up the birds. There were quite a lot of beaters, stretching right across the field to chase up the birds. That was great, we loved that.

When there was a fox hunt, you got off school. You told your teacher "Please, Miss, I'm going to a fox hunt." "That's all right, that's okay. Go to it." I think it was when the foxes were getting too many. They decided to try and reduce the population. We used to walk about and beat the brush with a stick, just the same as you did with the pheasants and grouse. It was mostly army officers, even foreigners on the guns. They shot a deer one day and my older brother along with some other boys got the job of tying the legs and carrying the deer down to Keltie castle. It was great fun.

My brother and I went to school in the village to start with, and then we went to Auchterarder. I was in his class in school. He was older than me and we were put in the same class. I don't know why that was, maybe a shortage of schoolteachers. It wasn't very good for my education, quite honestly.

There was a gardening class at school, and there was another chap, Joe. We won first prize in the gardening at Auchterarder school, quite a feat for two Glasgow lads.

Jemima (Forbes) Townsley: When we first came, we used to go to school in the afternoon and we used to pass the Dunning children, and they used to shout at us "Glasgow keelies". But we never had any fights, and we settled down. I got friendly with one girl, Janina Scott. I think her father was a shepherd.

But we evacuees did kind of keep together. Us going to separate classes, we never really mixed schoolwise with the Dunning people then. I remember Arthur Lothian, he was a nice boy, an evacuee. He had a sledge with a brake and we used to go down that hill at Mrs. Clark's farm. Mrs. Clark, she was very very kind to us. That was where Mrs. Macnab went to stay, and we used to go and visit her.

We left quite suddenly. My mother's house had got broken into in Glasgow and my mother decided "Oh, I think we better go home". My friend Janina, was off school with chickenpox, and I never saw her to say cheerio.

But we have never lost the love of the country we got here. I learned about leaves of trees. We got to know the birds, and my brother had a collection of eggs. He used to bring my mother a couple of rabbits and we had rabbit stew and things like that. We used to gather wood to burn in the fire. In Glasgow we always used coal.

My mother always said that the life we had in Dunning was what put us on our feet. We've all done quite well, the family. Maybe if we hadn't had that start here and got different values, maybe we wouldn't have done as well as we've done, we've all prospered. Just that wee background helped us.

Chapter 8: TWO GENERATIONS

Mrs. May (Brand) Hutchison and her mother Mrs. Margaret Brand, 1998

***Mrs. Margaret Brand is now over ninety. During World War II,
as an evacuee mum in Dunning, she turned from a city-dweller into
a real countrywoman. Her daughter May, who is now Mrs. Hutchison,
was inevitably raised in country ways.***

Mrs. Margaret Brand, Glasgow: My husband was Thomas Brand. My sons are
James and Thomas Brand, and my daughters are May and then Greta, who was born
in Dunning.

In 1939 we were living in Lauriston, Glasgow. On September third, we watched all
the evacuees leave the school. But I didn't like the idea of the children going, I
wanted them with me. My mother-in-law lived beside us, and I didn't want to leave
her.

My husband was working through in Perthshire and lived at Aberuthven, near
Dunning. He'd been in the army but was taken out to work for the Forestry
Commission. He worked at a sawmill for the chap Brown.

After the Clydebank blitz, my husband wrote and said he was getting us a place
called Rossie Cottage on the outskirts of Dunning. The children and I took the train.

Well, what a disappointment the cottage was---there was nothing in it! It belonged to Mr. Bell, the dairy farmer, and he let it out. To me it was just like a wee bothy, with very little furniture in it. We'd left a nice home in Glasgow.

The water was outside the door and there were no shops. I'm from the city. No shops! You had to walk from Rossie Cottage, I'd say a mile and a half, into Dunning for the groceries. Except for a Wednesday, when Mr. Laing came with his van. But on a Friday I would have to go in.

We thought it was terrible. May had just started school in Glasgow and Tommy was five, he was starting school in Dunning, and it was a long way especially for the two of them to walk to school.

May (Brand) Hutchison, Giffnock, Glasgow: I was born in Glasgow in February 1935. I remember a little of our being at Rossie Cottage outside Dunning. It was lovely countryside, and in my memory, it never rained. The sun shone every day and it seemed we were always able to go out and play. I remember hearing an aircraft and saying to my brother "It's one of ours." I don't know where we got that from. Or "That's a Spitfire". We didn't know what a Spitfire was, so we were obviously picking this up. We had some knowledge there was a war on.

I have very happy memories of Dunning and attending the village school, but the first year I can remember walking to Rossie, I was only five, it was winter and I was scared. For some reason my brothers weren't with me and I had to walk alone. Then we moved into the village.

Mrs. Margaret Brand: We stayed two or three months in Rossie Cottage. Then Mr. Brown must have spoken to his mother, and the minister came up to see me and said "I've got you a place right in Dunning".

Mr. Brown's mother owned the wee houses on Thimblerow, including the one we moved to. We were number 6 Thimble Row, and we were quite happy. There were two apartments. We had a bedroom and a sitting room where we put a bed. We sent for our own furniture and our own beds and I made it quite comfortable.

Running water? The wee tap was outside, shared with four other houses. And there were dry toilets. Mr. & Mrs. Campbell used to come and collect the dirt every Friday. What a carry on!

There was no gas or electricity, just paraffin lamps, and I had to cook on the coal fire, which was also the only heating we had.

Mrs. Brown came in and was talking about potato picking. We knew nothing about it, but James and Tommy and I went to lots of places: Dalreoch at the Broom, he was a posh farmer, and Scott at Millhaugh, and Peter Howie's farm and Alex Philip's. In the afternoons, coming in from the farms, the lorry left us all at Thimblerow and we came in and I had to start all the cooking.

My husband had moved to Thimblerow when we arrived. He continued working at Aberuthven and he and the chap Andrew Brown used to take their bicycles to go to work, at half past six in the morning.

Besides the potatoes, I worked at the threshing mill and the turnips. Mr. Howie said I would have made a good farmer's wife. I was up at the top of the threshing mill, working with the men. I had to go up and as the men forked the bundle of grain up to me, I picked it up, cutting the string with a knife strapped to my wrist and put it through the threshing mill. Never did that in my life! But you got used to it. Occasionally you'd cut yourself with the knife.

I worked at the farms when the weather was good. Then, starting from October, I worked with Mrs. Campbell at dressing the potatoes, putting them through the riddle. I worked on the farms for several years. I had never done that kind of work before, the only work I'd done in Glasgow was at a dairy. I'd been a lithographic printer up until I got married.

May (Brand) Hutchison: At the time I wasn't aware of it but with maturity, looking back, I feel I missed out on my primary education because I had two brothers, one two years older, one fifteen months younger, all in one class, segregated into rows.

When you think today that class size is no more than 32, our teacher must have had more than 50, all at different levels.

What we gained was a healthy lifestyle, a happy childhood, and we made lots of friends. I had no comparisons because I was too young to remember Glasgow. Because I was ten by then, it was more difficult for me coming back to Glasgow than it was going to Dunning. Going to Dunning was a happier change because I was young and adapted.

Mrs. Margaret Brand: Cycling from Aberuthven, my husband had an accident with a lorry on the main road. He was taken into the hospital at Auchterarder. The way he fell, his ankles were crushed. He was off work for close to two months and then he was okay. That's the worst thing which happened to us.

The Brand Family, post-war (1954). Back, L. To R. James, May, Tommy.
Front, L To R. Mr.Thomas Brand, Greta, Mrs. Margaret Brand

My sister came through to see us in Thimblerow, and the landlady said "Oh, you can stay for a night or two, no matter". My sister said "No way could I stay here, it's so quiet. She had to catch the last bus back to Glasgow that night. "I'd rather live with the bombs than live with the quietness here," she says. And she was very nervous, this sister of mine. She says "How are you going to manage?" and I says "Oh, we'll manage". She says "No gas or nothing, get me the last bus back!'

May (Brand) Hutchison: We were fully occupied between school and church. I remember going to church twice on a Sunday. I recall going down the road saying Genesis, Exodus, Leviticus…because if you didn't know that, you didn't get your wee text that you stuck in your Bible. This would be at Sunday School.

I picked raspberries somewhere. My father said we were going to make a fortune. We picked all day and made, I think, tuppence. The end of the first day, we all hid behind the door. When my father came home we whacked him with sticks, because he had said we were going to come in with a lot of money. And my grandmother, she was visiting us, she worked all day and didn't make any more than we did!

Mrs. Margaret Brand: I was young so there was nothing to the work, and I got used to it. But the first night on the potatoes, your back was broken. Mrs. Brown came in and she was laughing like hell. "You'll be all richt in the morning," she says, " You'll be all richt in the morning!" Next day the man came to say "Come away, Mrs. Brand". "Oh we couldna", I says. But we were okay.

I made quite a lot of friends in Dunning. Local people. And evacuees: there were quite a lot living with Jock the tailor when we arrived. But they left, the bombing was ended and the war seemed over, and I said "Well, Tommy is working, and we'll stay." And we did.

My life in Dunning was good. I would never have sampled it if it hadn't been for the war. I just got used to Dunning. When I visited Glasgow (because I never spent a Christmas in Dunning, I always used to go back to my own in Glasgow), the neighbour children were so white, and mine were all tanned. It did them a world of good.

Some of the residents grumbled about the evacuees. I don't know why, but the Dunning people were all so quiet and all of a sudden there's this bunch coming in with children, and the army coming in too. I suppose it would upset them, they were so used to their own way of living.

But the likes of Mrs. Brown, the landlady, she thought it was marvellous, she thought it livened up the village. So did Mrs. Laing, the grocer's wife. She could never understand why a lot of people used to grumble, and why they used to chase the children when they ran through the Square.

Jock the Tailor, he used to say it was a good thing, it was very sensible of us to have come away from Glasgow because we used to read in the papers about the raids. We thought we were lucky to be through in Dunning. He said that local people should be very thankful that they can help people like you coming into Dunning.

May (Brand) Hutchison: Most of my friends were evacuees, though I did make some friends in the village. One name I remember was Minnie Howie, who lived opposite Rossie Cottage. Marian Mitchell was one of the evacuees and the Donaldson twins were from Thornliebank in Glasgow.

My mother was expecting my young sister Greta and I told all and sundry where babies come from, much to the annoyance of Mrs. Donaldson, who appeared at the door that night, and asked if I was in. I was nine. I was told to say that the district nurse was bringing the baby in her black bag. Mrs. Donaldson told my mother that she objected to my giving her twins lessons in biology. I had to run and hide because it was "Wait till your father comes in". I hid in the dry toilet, in front of the house. I got a good talking to.

Mrs. Margaret Brand: I did have the hardest part, coming in, making the fire, cooking for them, giving the others theirs first, going out to fill up the jugs. This is what we missed the most, having the water outside, you couldn't get away from that.

Mrs. Brown used to give me the use of her wash-house out the back, and we hung the washing on the lines outside. We used a washing board, then put them through the wringer by hand. In Glasgow, we had had the steamies, the public wash-houses, which had driers and everything in them.

As the war was winding down, my husband was sent away from Aberuthven to work nearer Perth at Almondbank, to work at naval stores. He also cycled from Dunning to Almondbank, though it was ten miles. I always remember one Sunday the family was away with the church or something. It was a lovely day, and we walked from Thimblerow to Almondbank, and back again. He wanted to show me the place where he worked. (laughs) We were young, so nothing's a bother to you!

Greta and May Brand

May (Brand) Hutchison: I remember I always wanted a bicycle. We couldn't afford a bicycle. So we all had a gird. It was a bicycle wheel, and we had a stick, and we used to run through the village rolling along this gird. You used to hit it with your stick, it was as good as a bike.

We all played doublers, you know, balls. I played up the Park, I was in the Brownies, so it wasn't all just meeting in the hall, it was going out in the woods, with your arrows, your tracks. I was in the Brownies all the time I was in Dunning, and I loved it.

Mrs. Margaret Brand: I made friends, good friends, local people, in Dunning, including the Flockhart sisters, Mrs. Angus, Mrs. Howie up in Rossie Cottage. Belle Flockhart had a sweet shop, and she used to have to go in to Perth to get her stock every now and then. One day I was passing by, and her sister Margaret was in an invalid chair. Margaret shouted hello to me and when I went to speak to her the dog, a great big Alsation, went for me.

It went for my leg, and Margaret started screaming. The neighbours came out, and then the district nurse came by. She counted sixteen bites. The dog was shot. I was pregnant at the time with my daughter Greta.

May (Brand) Hutchison: When I go back to Dunning, I feel nostalgia for just about everything. I go back frequently. My sister was born there, and I remember wheeling the pram. I've taken my children back there. They're fed up listening to all the stories. It's a lovely part of Scotland, they agree, but it's not the same for them.

Mrs. Margaret Brand: We were among the last evacuees to leave Dunning. Greta was born July thirty-first, 1945 and we were back in Glasgow the next month when V-J Day was celebrated in George Square.

May (Brand) Hutchison: The best part of living in Dunning? The clean air, for a start, the food, everything. I thought it would always be like that. Since I came back to Glasgow I learned otherwise, but at the time I thought everybody had these things. That was why I was surprised I was sometimes singled out as a Glasgow keelie by the local kids. I was aware of something, but I couldn't put my finger on it. I guess I was experiencing prejudice, but I couldn't put a word to it. Just thinking "Why is she doing that?" and "Why did you say that?" because I'm just like you, I mean we're all just children.

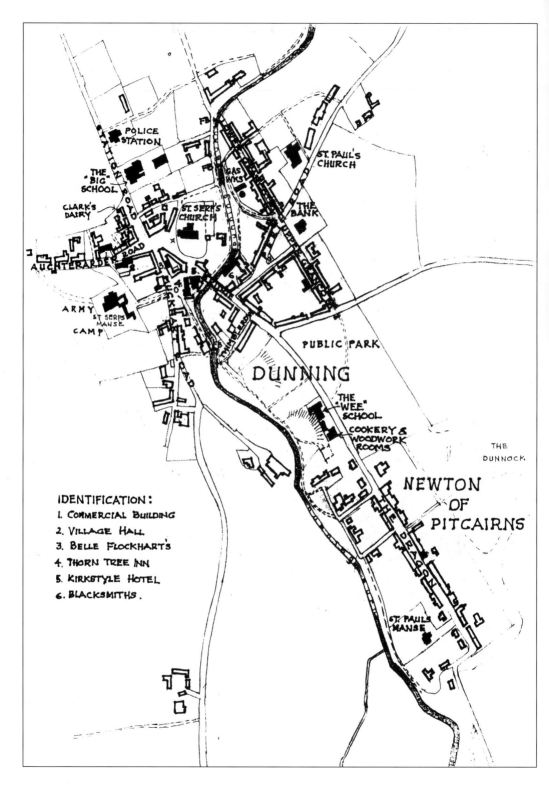

Dunning Village, circa 1939

Chapter 9: THE VILLAGE INFLUENCE

The experience for other city children of living in a country setting made in some cases a lasting impression. Here are the stories of three such lifelong influences.

Bill Smith lives now in Spateston, Johnstone

Bill Smith: I arrived at Alexandra Park Station in Glasgow with my mother, my brother and my sister to take the train to Dunning, though I'm not sure we knew where we were going. I was nine, my brother Eric was just a year younger than me, and my sister was only four at the time. That's the reason my mother came along, because if there was a child under school age then the mother could come with the family. My father was in the air force.

Eric & Bill Smith head for the Dunning Burn

We were billeted in Thorntree Villa with a Miss Mailer, an older lady. We stayed there a year or maybe less. Then we moved into the famous Commercial Buildings on Auchterarder Road opposite the Village Hall.

We arrived September third, 1939, the day war was declared and we remained here until the end of the war, August 1945.

Highlights? There are many highlights. The whole family lived here, we had visitors come up, father came up on leave for weekends. We had uncles come up, they were in the air force as well. When the Blitz was on in Glasgow we had people come up. We could see the Blitz from here. We could hear the guns, see the searchlights, hear the planes.

I can remember troops coming back from Dunkirk, with virtually nothing. They stayed in the field behind the manse. There were all sorts of soldiers here during the war but the ones who stick in my mind were those from Dunkirk. There was a lot of poor souls there, I can tell you. They were coming out without rifles or anything and the story was that they had to pay for the equipment they'd left on the beaches. That was the story anyway.

I went to primary school here in Dunning, then to Auchterarder. Later, my brother and I both went to Perth Academy for three years.

Being here was a tremendous experience. As a town lad I worked at harvest, at the potato and berry picking. We worked on the estates at grouse-shooting, pheasant-shooting, deer hunts. I worked at the Quilts farm every Saturday morning for two to two and a half years at the inside threshing mill making cattle-feed. Quilts Farm is a mile up the hill on the Yetts o' Muckhart Road. Half an hour going up, five minutes coming down. I think I used to get something like five shillings or half a crown, and half a dozen eggs, a bottle of milk, and every so often a chicken. And you had your dinner up there before you left.

Bill & Eric Smith as Dunning tattie howkers

The whole family were really naturalised Dunningites, if you like, when we left. I lived here from age nine to fifteen and my youngest brother was born here, in Perth Infirmary, around about VE Day in May of 1945.

My mother was an evacuee helper along with Mrs. Agnes Clark in Oswald Villa. She also went to work with Fentons' at potato dressing. She was also the Prudential insurance agent in the village.

It was a good experience being here. I was "Digging for Victory" during the war. My brother and I both had plots behind what was then the police station. That started off my interest in horticulture. Then it was all veg. We grew potatoes, leeks, onions and lettuce. And we showed at the village show. I think 1945 was the first horticultural society show. The main thing I can remember there was Wilson the roadman with these big leeks which stretched across two tables. He grew them in drainpipes, fantastic leeks.

That gardening started my interest in horticulture. Now I'm vice-chairman of the Scottish National Chrysanthemum and Dahlia Society. I've been a committee member there since 1970 and I've shown all over Scotland and the north of England. I've won gold medal for best vase in the national show, and some of the cups there. That interest in growing things started right here in Dunning when I was an evacuee.

Bill Smith with an award winning vase of dahlias at a Scottish National show

Living in the countryside also left its stamp on George Alexander, who lives now in Auchinsarry, Kilsyth:

I was 11 when war started. I came from a big family but there were only two of us at home when war was declared, my sister and myself.

The school I was attending needed room, so I was sent to Haghill School, and it was mostly those pupils who were evacuated here. I was evacuated with them, but I didn't actually come to Dunning in the first instance. I went to Auchterarder. I stayed there for...I can't remember how long, a few months I think...and then I came to Dunning.

In Dunning I stayed at Broadslap farm, with the Kirk family. I continued going to Auchterarder School.

I wasn't afraid being evacuated. I don't think I had very much feeling at all. It was just an adventure. I think we were under the impression that they were going to issue us with arms, so we could shoot the Germans.

The funny thing was that we didn't miss our family. I don't recollect being homesick or anything like that. We'd a jolly good time here.

We got up to all the mischief that young lads do, and we had of course lots of freedom. We had some good friends with the local people…Jimmy Scott up the Dragon, and his auntie Mrs. Kettles. Lots of them were very good. They didn't make us feel like interlopers, they accepted us.

I can remember we bought an old motorbike for ten bob (fifty pence of new money!) Several of us boys had to club together for this motorbike. We used to race this thing up the hills and all over until…I'm afraid we didn't know you needed to put oil into it…the dashed thing seized up, fell to pieces.

I was at Broadslap about a year and a half, and then I went back to Glasgow to finish school.

My wife and I have four children and seven grandchildren. The children at our local school did an evacuee project, you know a war project, and we were quizzed on what we did during the war. I had to tell them my experience, what I did when I was a wee laddie, and then what I did when I was in the services. I was in the services from 1949-59. The children wanted to know what games we played, what games we had, like soldiers and castles and bicycles and rollerskates.

Then when we came here for the first Evacuees' Reunion we had schools to visit. We went to Blackford School, and the kids there were doing a project on the war. We had great questions from them, intelligent questions, and they kept in touch with us after, sending us letters asking more questions. Food was one of the things they asked about. They had been told about ration books. And they asked how we managed for food, and did we have sweets. We did have sweets, but that was only the first day or two after you got the ration, then that was it until the next ration.

Before I started my apprenticeship as a coachbuilder, I came back here for a while and worked at Broadslap farm. Lots of great excitement then, especially at the threshing mills, when we went out to help the various farmers. You know, each farmer had help from all the farmers round about. I remember one threshing mill we were at, and I can't even remember the farmer's name. He seems to have been a very mean kind of character. After working all day carrying the grain---it was in huge bags, really heavy bags, and we were only youngsters at the time and we were carrying this grain up the steps into the granary at the top---he handed us a shilling at the end of the day. That was our wage. And apparently, I can't remember this but I'm assured this is what I did, I threw the shilling into the horse trough, and told him he could keep his.....shilling. And I'm told that he was in there up to his arms getting the shilling, and I never got it back. (laughs)

When the war ended, we'd somehow managed to get a few thunderflashes from the Home Guard. Those are loud noise-making devices that weren't dangerous but were used in military exercises to simulate explosions. I don't know how we got them, but as the war's end was being celebrated, we were throwing them all over the place. We threw them up one of the pends, and they were reverberating inside the pend. I discovered that I was the only one there, and the next thing I knew, there was a big boot up my backside. The policeman, Black Jock, he had me by the scruff of the neck, and he booted me along the road.

There was a lion fountain along the road, and I can remember someone trying to put a thunderflash, they were tubular things, up the mouth of the lion, and setting them off. Oh, we weren't popular that night. It was a celebration, but I think we were a bit of a nuisance.

I think the experience here made us appreciate country life. Staying in Glasgow and then coming out here, you know, we had lots of freedom. Since then I suppose we've never wanted to stay in a town again. Even though we were staying in a housing estate, we were always wanting away, and eventually we got a place with a piece of ground and plenty of room to stretch out. I think that was the grounding we had when we were evacuated.

Walter Steel lives now in Stockport outside Manchester. His years in Dunning as an evacuee gave him a lifetime hobby.

Walter Steel: I was born June twenty-eighth, 1928, and I lived on Marwick Street, Denistoun, Glasgow.

When we left on the evacuation train, we felt great. It was just an adventure to us. My friends were all together, and each of us had a bag of food, gas mask, a label round our neck. All in line, chattering like mad. We didn't know where we were going. We had no idea. We carried bags of food. Mine had enough food to keep me going for 48 hours, a can of corned beef, biscuits, that sort of thing. And a bar of plain chocolate, which I hated. (Laughs) I suppose, it was enough, when you landed on someone's house, you had at least forty eight hours food to keep you going till the other people got organised and settled in.

There were seven children in our family, and I was the youngest by far. I was 11, my next sister up was seven years older than me, and it went on from there.

I was in Dunning for three years. And I can honestly say that they were three of the happiest years I've had in my life. I had a lot of freedom there.

We were all allocated to houses. How it was done, I don't know. There were six of us ended up in the bank. (It's not the bank now, it's a house at the corner of Perth road and the Upper Granco). We were all boys of the same age. It was a big house. Somebody must have come around and said "How many rooms have you got? Oh you can take six."

The banker wasn't very happy having us there. We were there two or three months, that's all. We weren't ill-treated, but it was a frosty atmosphere. I wasn't homesick, I don't know why. We had to write home regularly, which was a good thing.

I went to school up the Dragon, in a big hall. There was a teacher who came from Glasgow, she taught us. It wasn't a strict school. Let's face it, the teacher was there out of sufferance, from Glasgow. She just did the minimum, so we had a lot of freedom. I was probably a year at that school, and then I went on to Auchterarder.

Talking about education, I realised afterwards that my education had really suffered, being away from Glasgow. I could compare, coming back to Glasgow, how much I'd slipped. Because the Auchterarder school was bursting at the seams with its own population, and then all the evacuees going in there. Yes, the classes were pretty full, and there was a shortage of teachers as well. Half of them were in the army. I really had to knuckle down when I came back to Glasgow, but I think I still didn't quite make the grade I would have had I stayed in Glasgow all the time. But you catch up. And I'm still here!

It didn't take the banker long to farm us out to other people. I went to a house on the Lower Granco Street, next to the gasworks. I used to watch the guy hauling out the red-hot coke, hosing it down, making the gas, and filling up the big tank. Very few houses in Dunning had electricity at that time. Ours had, but all the rest had gas lamps and paraffin lamps.

It was the Chalmers family with whom I lived, a brother and two sisters. Another boy who was there left soon after, and I stayed on. I was with them a long time. Tom Chalmers I think was a doctor. One sister was an ex-nurse, and the other was a schoolteacher.

On the road to Auchterarder, on the left hand side, there was a large estate called Keltie. The people were away to war, and there was an old gamekeeper left in charge. Whether it was his nephew, I don't know, but I got very friendly with this lad who was staying with him. I spent lot of time on that estate. I would just get my bike out, and away to see him.

My friend's name was Wilf James. He was a bit older than me. He used to be quite interested in electrics. He used to get old valves and try to make radios and stuff like that. He wanted a shop of his own.

We didn't work with the gamekeeper, but he taught us how to handle guns. I wouldn't say we had free range of the guns, but he'd give us a .22 rifle and we'd shoot rabbits and things like that. Not many lads that age would get that chance.

I well remember Keltie estate. There was a small pond, and a big one, with a boathouse. We tried fishing in that big pond, but we didn't catch anything. The small pond used to freeze over in the winter, and we used to skate on it. We used the old-fashioned skates, clamps that screwed onto your shoes.

When you think about it, we were dicing with death. That ice could have broken and we could have, shunnkhh, gone down, just like that.

You know the little stream that goes through Dunning, the burn? That's where I learned how to fish. I started off with a long elderberry stick, and that was no use, it kept breaking. So I got a long bamboo pole and a line on it. Tom Chalmers went to Perth and got me a nine foot rod. And a reel. I've still got it. A Greenheart rod. And I fished that burn. I went to Forteviot on my bike and fished in the River May---that was a good river for catching fish. That's what started me into fishing. And the bug's still there. I'm still fishing.

You see, Dunning was a complete contrast to Glasgow. Glasgow was all cement streets and what have you. Whereas, Dunning? Country. Wildlife. Fishing. Shooting. Running wild.

My brother had given me an old second-hand bike. Bikes were hard to come by. The first bike we got was old-fashioned and had no brakes. We screwed another saddle on the cross bar and whoever sat on that had to do all the pedalling. So there were two of us on it, and there were no brakes. You had to put your foot on the front tire to stop it. But you could do things like that in a small village like Dunning, there were no cars.

Potato picking, that was really hard work. But then, boys are full of bravado: "We can earn some money here". We used to get picked up in the morning, in a van, boys, women, girls, men as well, and we'd be taken to this farm. Depending on how many were there, the farmer would pace out a drill. You divide them into bits. "Are you going to do a bit, or half a bit?"

The horse and the machine would come down, throwing out the potatoes. You're bent down and you've got to pick them all, at a certain speed, because the horse and machine will come round and come down again. And if he's got to stop because you're still picking, you get shouted at. To start with, your back is killing you, absolutely killing you. You don't get a chance of straightening, you're down there and it gets so bad you're down on your knees 'Oh, get those potatoes up".

I'd never do it again. I did it two years on the trot, and the funny thing is that your back gets so used to bending like that, towards the end it's no problem at all. You're down there, not on your knees and you're whish whish whish getting all those potatoes into the skulls, getting them away. No problem! But to start with, your back…oh, it's not funny! Yes, we did that a couple of years to get pocket money.

We used to have some hard winters. Cold. One winter it really snowed and the Station Road was completely blocked off. They cut a track through, just wide enough for one car. Well, stupid boys, of course, "Oh, let's go and see this." We went tootling down with our bikes, with a car coming the other way. There was no way we could pass, just drive straight into the snow. That's the kind of thing that boys do, girls wouldn't do that.

My family came up every so often and I went down to Glasgow once or twice, not very often. Once in Glasgow I went down---it was just after an air raid. My brother had a motorbike and he took me down to see the damage. It was quite horrific, you know, for a young lad to see these tenement blocks just sliced like that, schunnk. All the furniture in the rooms just sitting there. I'll never forget that, and the curtains blowing in the wind. That was my only experience of the effects of the bombing.

I was amazed when I first came back and saw how small the Dunning Burn was. Of course as an eleven year old boy, it seemed quite big, you know, and you go back "God, did I fish in that?" but there were trout there. Small things, we used to catch them. And eels. I didn't guddle for eels, I was frightened of that, but I guddled for trout though.

When you're guddling for trout, you've got to be very gentle. You've got to use your hands. You got to know where the trout is, or think you know where a trout

is, under a stone or under a bank. And you gradually work your hand down. You feel a trout, and as soon as you feel you've got it whhiik you whip it up on the bank quick. And the trout, surprisingly, will stay there. It'll feel you working your fingers round it. Sometimes it goes away. But very often it will stay there, and you'll whip it out. That's guddling.

Or you can snare them. You get a little thin bit of wire, like a snare, put it around it "krrickk" and snare them. I did that sometimes. And we snared rabbits. Sold them to the butcher for tenpence each. That was pocket money. I suppose for the butcher, during the war, food was rationed and that was a bit extra for him. So we used to buy these snares, hang them on fences where the rabbits ran through. In the fields, woods, anywhere at all around the village, and we very often caught them. Tenpence each, that was big money!

I used to snare with other boys, I think maybe some of them might have been locals. I don't recall any animosity with the locals. There were no fights or anything like that.

All boys get up to tricks like stealing apples. I remember once, half way up the Dragon, we looked down at this garden and saw all these apple trees there. There were two or three of us in between the rows with big canes, knocking apples off. And up on the wall, was the policeman standing and watching us. As soon as we saw him whoosht we scampered. He knew fine as soon as we saw him we'd be off.

They were three happy years. The funny thing is you tend to remember the happy times and forget the bad times. There must have been bad times, but I forget them. I've no regret that I went there, none at all. Not one bit.

Chapter 10: THE EVACUEE WHO STAYED

Les McColl, 1994

***In 1993, when the Dunning Parish Historical Society first decided to research
the subject of World War II evacuees, we knew of the whereabouts of only one
surviving evacuee, Les McColl. Here's his story:***

Leslie McColl, Dunning: My name is Leslie McColl. I was born September
twenty-second, 1932, so I wasn't quite seven when the war started. This is the tag I
got as an evacuee:

GOVERNMENT EVACUATION SCHEME
CITY OF GLASGOW

NAME McCOLL   LESLIE
(IN BLOCK CAPITALS)

ADDRESS F2 WALTER ST.
                              E 1

DATE OF BIRTH (If Child) 18.9.32.

SCHOOL ATTENDED HAGHILL

On the other side it describes Haghill School, at the bottom of Walter Street, where
I stayed, as the Assembly School where we were to gather. The government had this
thing going, in the event of war, to evacuate all Glasgow children.

When the war started on the third of September, the police came up, rung a bell, and told everyone to go to Haghill School for the evacuation.

I didn't have brothers and sisters, and I stayed with my grandmother and grandfather. My mother died when I was two. My father was in the Air Force and he was killed.

I remember my grandfather taking me down the steps. He was trying to take my hand to the school, but I didn't want to know. My two pals across the road came out and the three of us went down ourselves. We got into the playground, I was number 6 assembly point. I can remember them checking my label, checking my gas mask. You had to take your gas mask out of this cardboard box, wave it about and put it back in. And you had a wee bag of sandwiches.

I said cheerio to my family, aunties and various people who were all round the railings at Haghill School. We got marched across the road to Alexandra Park Station and were put in the train. I distinctly remember the railway man going right along the train. There weren't any corridors in trains in those days, and he locked the doors, with a big brass key.

We actually thought we were going away up to the Highlands: that's what I was led to believe. In fact, I thought we'd be running about with kilts and swords. With your imagination at that age, you think things that you read in books are going to happen.

I can remember getting to Dunning, getting on these blue buses, and coming up to the village and into the school. I think the system was if you had any spare rooms in your house, they sort of commandeered them, these billeting officers.

This farmer from the Broom, he'd asked the billeting officer to send him three lads. I think he was just wanting us to work, he wasn't interested in evacuees. Away we went to the Broom, the three of us pals. Eddie Bishop and Andy Shaw were quite a bit bigger than me. When the farmer saw me, I was that small he says "Oh naw, no way, I don't want you." But as a matter of fact I was the leader of the gang.

So I says "If you don't take me, you don't take naebody". So I mind this man passing on a pushbike and I says to him "Where's the road to Glasga, mister?" And he says "Doon there, laddie." So I says "Ah well, that'll do me. Right Eddie, let's go." So away we went.

I don't think we got even a quarter of a mile and this car drew up and a policeman was in it. And he says "Where're you going, boys?" I says "Glasga." "Naw naw you're not. Get in here." So he brought us back to Dunning School.

They split the three of us up. The other two got sent to various places, and I was the last one in the school. It was one of the billeting officers, Mr. Francie Winton, who took me. I stayed with them until 1944. The way things turned out, I was very lucky. They took me as one of the family, and the relations still do to this day.

The evacuation was okay for a fortnight and then the novelty wore off. The bombing hadn't started at that time, so everybody started dribbling back home. Some of the parents of the evacuees came and took them back.

I was wanting out of here, too. I was a bit fed up. But one thing in its favour, we didn't have a school to go to so we only spent about half a day in a class. And then we ended up in the cookery, in the woodworking classroom. They made that into a class but it was very small, considering that something like 300 evacuees came here.

We never fitted in here in Dunning, the evacuees. There were the Dunning folk and there was us. Even in school, we were separated. After some of them went home, then we got on, but it took a long time. We were known as Glasgow keelies. That's what they called us, Glasgow keelies.

We called them teuchters, the local people. I'm not sure what it means, but we called them teuchters, and they called us Glasgow keelies. Even to this day, people will say to me, "Who are you?" "I'm Les McColl". "Oh, you're Francie Winton's refugee." That was the older people in the village, so I mean there's still that bit there. A refugee! Really an evacuee but they called you a refugee.

It was different I think for people that came with their families, because they eventually got houses of their own. Whereas if you were alone as an evacuee, you stayed an evacuee.

But as I say I was very fortunate. The government scheme provided that when you had an evacuee staying with you, you got seven shillings a week: the government paid you to keep them. The day I left Mrs. Winton gave me a bank book. She'd saved every seven shillings she got from the government, and she gave it to me the day I left. That old farmer at the Broom who turned me down because of my size did me a real favour.

A lot of evacuees had good places, and a lot of them had bad places. Most of the farmers wanted people to work, a sort of free labour system, and that put a lot away. They didn't want to work on the farms, so they wrote to their parents and told them to get them back.

Mr. Winton had a haulage business, so I spent most of the time going about the area in a lorry. That's how I knew everybody so well, because grocers, everybody, had to get things through this haulage business. Then after Dunkirk, the army confiscated the lorries, so Mr. Winton took up trapping for a living. That was right up my street. Trapping, shooting, fishing, these were my good times here! Never would have happened if I'd stayed in Glasgow.

When I was an evacuee in Dunning there was an old guy we used to call the old Canadian. It was dry toilets in those days; very few people in Dunning had flush toilets. Anyway, he had this garden down the alleyway, and there was an old lady lived in a cottage on the alley. He used to go in and visit her. He used to take his pails from the dry toilet up to the garden and put it in the garden for manure. This day he left his pails sitting at her door, and I had a tyre to play with as a gird, just a wheel you know. Well my tyre hit the pails and knocked one of them in her door. So the old guy chased me for years and years…he even took a gun to me at one time.

The people I stayed with, as I said, ended up trapping and shooting. And I had a gun as well. Their house was straight across the burn from this old Canadian's garden. He had eight or nine beehives. And I used to wait until he was out of the road, and blow the beehives up. (laughs)

I left here in 1944. I had written to my granny and told her that I wanted to get out of here. There was always that bit that I wanted to get back to Glasgow. It's part of life, I guess, you never forget where you were born and brought up. An aunt of mine put me in a boarding school in England. Anyway, I definitely didn't fit in there…a wee straw hat and a blazer sort of set-up! For a boy from Denistoun in Glasgow, you just dinna do these things!

So I came back to Glasgow, went to Whitehill School and then I left. In those days you left then when you were fourteen. I came back to Dunning for a couple of months, and since I was getting on to fifteen, I decided I wanted to join the army. I was away nine years.

The time I was away all my family went to America and Australia, so when I came back I had no place to stay in Glasgow. I came and stayed with the Wintons in Dunning, and that's when I met my wife Ina, Ina McLeish.

We got married in Glasgow, and I had a job in the docks. A great job, but they went on strike twice a week, for months. They emptied the Clyde of ships! So I came back to Dunning, got a flat above the Wintons' house, and just stayed here in the village ever since.

Ina and Les McColl on their wedding day

*Former teacher Barbara (Kaye) Peacock and the McCabe
sisters describe their evacuee experiences to pupils at
Forteviot school during the 1994 Evacuees' Reunion*

Chapter 11: THE GIRLS OF INVERMAY

For the three McCabe sisters evacuated to Dunning from Glasgow, the highlight was eventually being billeted at nearby Invermay Estate.

Before the war: Christine, Sarah and May McCabe

May McCabe (now Mrs. McCusker, of Rothesay):   I was 11 years old in the summer of 1939. Before the schools broke up there was a buildup to war. For the summer holidays we had gone to Rothesay on the Isle of Bute to be with our grandparents. Then we had to return quickly to Glasgow. We had to queue, like you've seen old pictures of people queuing to leave France on the last boat. Most of the ships, the steamers, were being commandeered for the war effort.

Sunday, September third, before my mother, my two sisters and my brother and I set off on the train, I remember my main concern was how my father was going to cope without us all. I think I was a bit snivelly although I was the oldest. I maybe had a clearer picture of what the situation was, although I was still pretty young for my age at that time. I think I cried for a long time in the train, and I felt embarrassed because I was obviously the oldest but the one that was doing most of the crying.

Christine McCabe (now Mrs. Melville, of Rothesay):   I'm the middle of the McCabe sisters. I was ten when we left. I thought it was great fun being evacuated: we were coming to the country and that was it. We were lucky to have our mother come with us, because we had a younger brother, Robert, aged three and a half. That was the rule, she had to come because my brother was under five

When we got to Dunning, nobody wanted to know us. They wanted to split us, because we were a family of five. My mother just held out until they found somewhere for us.

In the end, we went to the Perth road, to an older couple. They really didn't have room for us. We were there only a matter of weeks, because it wasn't safe. My mother had only a small open fire to cook on, in the sitting room. I think that was where she and Robert slept, and we girls slept upstairs. A pot of boiling soup spilled on my brother's foot. It was a very bad burn. It was treated locally by the district nurse, but that was it, and they had to find us some place more suitable.

Sarah McCabe (now Mrs. Murray, of Glasgow): I was eight and a half. I was quite sad when we had to come away to Dunning. There was all that hustle bustle and here you were with tags tied around you and gas masks. I cried even though my mother was with me. My feeling was that everybody else was getting away to billets and homes and we were left standing about. I wasn't very happy about the situation.

In fact I wasn't very happy at all coming to Dunning. I felt a lot of the people didn't like us. I felt we were resented in lots of ways by some people. When we went to the first house we stayed in I felt she particularly didn't like us. I think she felt snobbish towards us. She must have volunteered to have us, but she didn't seem to like us at all. I felt she wasn't a very nice person.

May (McCabe) McCusker: We finally moved to Burnside Cottage up the Dragon. I remember going into this lovely cottage, right next to the burn, and going out into the garden which had a bit of an orchard. There were all the windfalls from the apple trees and the pear trees. The burn, we loved that, the freedom in the water and the stepping stones, and getting ourselves wet, like you do as children. And I can always smell that autumn morning in that garden.

Christine (McCabe) Melville: I don't remember much until we moved to the wee school up the hill where Miss Haggart was our only teacher. Other Glasgow teachers came with us but they seemed to disappear, and she stayed with us. I thoroughly enjoyed school. Even Miss Haggart---I got on well with her. Everybody seemed to think she was a bit grumpy but I liked Miss Haggart.

Sarah (McCabe) Murray: I didn't like Miss Haggart because previously my two sisters were taught by her and if I did anything wrong she would say "Your sisters wouldn't do things like that". My brother was in an even worse position, he had three sisters ahead.

May (McCabe) McCusker: Our family moved to the Commercial Buildings. We had a little more accommodation. My mother had a kitchen cum living room, with a very old fashioned bed. We also had a very big kitchen range you had to black lead. They were marvellous those kitchen ranges, you could cook so many things on them. The soup would be going and my mother, when she was able to get the ingredients, was able to make madeira cake, which was a great treat.

It was exciting because at that time all the soldiers were billeted in the village. They were up by the Manse. We used to go round to their cookhouse and get bits of their rations.

Christine (McCabe) Melville: My father fell ill, and my mother went back to Glasgow to look after him and took my brother with her. When he turned five he came back to Dunning, and stayed at what was then the dairy.

The three of us sisters went to Invermay estate, which lies between Dunning and Forteviot, in 1942. It was wonderful. There were about forty girls, from 5 to 14. We were split up into age groups. We weren't separated as such, but you were known as the babies, the juniors and whatever. We slept in dormitories, and each of us slept with our own age group. It was like having thirty-eight sisters instead of just two. The older ones looked out for us juniors, and we looked out for the little ones.

We used to come on weekends to Dunning to see our brother. It was one of those times when we were really happy. We were well cared for. It was Guiders, senior Girl Guide leaders, who looked after us. They were marvellous.

May (McCabe) McCusker: Winter was a special time in places like Invermay. There was a wee loch… that's what it looked to us as children at the foot of the Ochil Hills up there on the estate…but it was probably a pond, and that's where some of the families did their curling.

They had a great big walled garden which was neglected. We managed to climb over to it. There were plum trees and apple trees and fruit that seemed to be going to waste. We were greedy in situations like that, and this garden was a great attraction for us.

We were all Brownies or Guides and that kept us busy, and we still kept links with our colleagues the Guides and Brownies in Dunning. We'd come into Dunning quite often, running down the road and sneaking down to the chip shop.

Sarah (McCabe) Murray: Invermay was absolutely wonderful. We were all divided into groups, each with its room, and each room had the name of a ship. I think we were disciplined quite a bit. I think I would feel it, because my two sisters always said I was spoiled. Christmases were wonderful. We had a huge playroom, and when we were let into it on Christmas morning, the Christmas tree stretched to the ceiling, and the presents we got were out of this world. The Americans had sort of adopted us and we got lots of stuff sent from America. We had beautiful dresses, dungarees. Because Invermay was a big estate we were always outdoors and up trees so we got dungarees.

The House at Invermay Estate, between Forteviot and Dunning
(Valentine photo courtesy of St. Andrews University Library)

Christine (McCabe) Melville: Walking through the woods in Invermay in the winter was magical. Amid all the trees it didn't seem cold. It was absolutely beautiful. I don't think I've ever been anywhere like that since, and I've been a lot of places.

My brother had not been long at the dairy in Dunning when my parents discovered the children were not being well cared for. He was moved to a boys' hostel in the village of Stanley about 15 miles away and so he was really separated from us then. My parents used to come down to see us regularly, and they picked up Robert first before coming to see us. We kept in touch.

May (McCabe) McCusker: We were quite lucky. We had our own cook, Mrs. Potter. Some of the food was horrible and you just had to sit at the table and try to finish it but the other food was great. I still remember some of this food with great affection and have tried to make it for ourselves. Particularly there was a fish pie which my sisters hated, and there was a ham and bacon and bean pie which I used to love, and then a great big ginger steak pudding and things like that. Big scones for Sunday tea.

Sarah (McCabe) Murray: Every day we had to walk from Invermay to the village school in Forteviot. Soldiers were billeted in the grounds doing manoeuvres. We had beautiful packed lunches with us and we used to give the soldiers some of our lunches and we'd get cakes and chocolate in return. They always lined up when we were walking down that avenue, and Miss Kaye, our teacher, cycled to school and they always said "Good morning, Miss Kaye" as she went through us. It was a good happy time.

May (McCabe) McCusker: We had a big playroom and there was a conservatory. My dormitory was at the front of the house. I can remember looking at the stars from the big windows. Invermay had a great tree on the lawn and a swing, and I used to lie down there and write poetry.

Sarah (McCabe) Murray: Invermay was really a happy time. It's a beautiful house, the grounds are gorgeous. We were quite hard workers and we helped pick potatoes. We went to a farm on Station Road to pick potatoes. We were paid for it, and the money was put into an account for us. We picked potatoes, shawed the turnips. I was always crying because I didn't like the cold. I didn't always cry but I did when the frost was on the ground and my hands were cold.

May (McCabe) McCusker: There was also the home farm at Invermay. It was just up the road. In those days the farm…how can I put it…to us it seemed an awfully dirty smelly place, not like farms are now. We got very friendly with the man who looked after the cows and his wife. It seemed they were so poor. I remember when this lady had a wee baby and we were all delighted. I went down to Invermay House and found a bit of material and sewed it up into a bib for this wee baby. It sticks in my mind that they were so poor. Maybe it was because we were staying in this big airy house. They always had to work hard, and it seemed to us almost a hovel they were staying in, it was so dark and dismal.

When I went to the high school in Perth, we had to get up earlier in the morning than all the others, have our cocoa for breakfast and our porridge, and then go trekking down to Forteviot station. We'd kick our heels until the train came, and, for the few pennies we'd have, there was a hotel there and we'd go to the back door and buy some biscuits. At school we always had to leave just that bit early, about twenty minutes to four, to get the train to go back again. Then we had to walk up, summer and winter to the big house. It didn't matter if the snow was up to your waist, you trudged up, pitch black at night, because there were no lights.

We used to occasionally pinch the odd turnip out of the fields, knock the top off it and eat this coming up the road.

Christine (McCabe) Melville: Looking back on the nearly five years I spent in the area, I thoroughly enjoyed it. When people talk now about the war, I had a good war. We never heard an air raid or anything and we thoroughly enjoyed it.

May (McCabe) McCusker: Yes, Invermay spoiled us for later on in life. You got accustomed to living in this big estate and you almost felt it belonged to you. It was always there, in the back of your mind, as you were growing up. Invermay was a special place, there's no doubt about it.

The Second Influx

Helen (Flannagan) Mann & brother Jack Flannagan describe to Patricia Wallace the spot where Granny Huttton's cottage once stood, and where they stayed as evacuees.

Chapter 12: JUST DROPPED US OFF

Most World War II evacuees arrived in rural Britain in organised school groups. Jack and Helen Flannagan and their mother arrived in less orthodox fashion.

Jack Flannagan, Cumbernauld: I was born on December 30th, 1930, in Govan. We moved from there to Maryhill, the other side of town, when I was about five. That was us going up in life. My father was brought up in Govan...he was four when they left Ireland. My mother and grandmother were Irish too.

My father was a mad red-haired Irishman and very quick-tempered. He had a great sense of humour, played practical jokes on everybody, and funny enough, could take a practical joke. Normally somebody that plays a practical joke can't take a joke back but if it was really funny he enjoyed it.

He was born in 1899. When the Great War started in 1914, he wanted to go to the war. But of course he was too young. So he told a lie about his age and was in France driving a double-decker bus when they discovered his age. For real devilment they kept him in the army till 1922. He was in trouble in Ireland with the IRA in Dublin. He came out of the army, met and married my mum, and they had three children.

War broke out in 1939. I think at first my mum and dad were quite anxious to get us out of the town. But then again I suppose like most parents they didn't want to part with their children. I always remember my mother's words that day. We were all ready to go. It was a tenement building we stayed in and we were out on the stair with all the other families. Right down the stair you could hear all the talking going on, we were in the top flat. And my mum just decided there and then "You're not going" she said. "If we're going to die we're all going to die together."

We stuck it out until I think it was 1941 when bombs started dropping all over the damn place. My mum decided "I think we should get out of town". There was talk for a wee while and then my dad came up with the idea. He must have told my mum to get everything ready. He didn't tell us children what he was doing, it was between my mother and father you see. He was a lorry driver. He decided that one day he was going to come up to Perth and Dundee with his lorry.

One day he just threw all the cases and things onto the lorry and put my mum and Helen and I into the cab of the lorry and he drove up to Dunning. Catherine, my oldest sister, she stayed in town. She was seven years older than me and she was working then in the hospital. She probably thought "I'm too big a girl to get evacuated."

It was a Saturday when dad brought us up, I can't remember the date or anything. It was an adventure to me, coming up to Dunning. My dad knew where he was going. He was a lorry driver all his days, so he knew roads existed that weren't on maps. I don't know whether he knew Dunning or whether he had passed through it once or twice. Anyway he knew where it was. He brought us up here, and I'm afraid he had to rush away. He more or less dropped us off at the top of the street. There was a lady at the top of the street, I guess my mother talked to her and we stayed in her house that night, sleeping on the floor.

We got up the next morning and we didn't have any breakfast. The lady in the house didn't have anything. Of course everything was rationed.

Helen and I went out. My mum says "See if you can find some shops." It was Sunday morning, and Dunning…I don't know whether it's still the same…it's a ghost town, isn't it, Sunday morning? We went out and there were two soldiers. Soldiers had taken over the whole village, the place was littered with guns. The Royal Artillery was here and their trucks were all over the one side of the Granco, with camouflage netting all over them.

These two soldiers were changing a tyre, and I asked them where the shops were. This guy asked me, "Speak again" he says. "What do you mean, speak again?" He says "You've got a Glasgow accent". And I says "I'm from Glasgow. Maryhill". And he says "So am I. Whereabouts in Maryhill?" "Rolland Street". "Ah" he says, "I know Rolland Street, I stay in Stair Street" he says. And I says to him "I know Stair Street, I pass it going to school in the morning." And he says "What school do you go to?" I says "St. Charles's". He says "St. Charles's. You'll be one of those wee Catholickers then." "Yes" I says.

And I found out afterward he was called 'Sash', because he was an Orangeman and he wore one of those sashes. Later we became good friends. In the war I don't think religion entered into anything. There was no bigotry in the war at all, I think, thank God.

Anyway we started talking to one another and he asks "What are you looking for?" and I says "Well, we've no messages at all, nothing to eat". I suppose maybe he stole the damn stuff but he drove us to his cookhouse in the camp which was out past the village hall. He had to cover us up with a coat in the truck because we shouldn't be seen in the camp in the truck. And he brought sugar, tea, butter, not a lot of it, but enough to get us by. Milk, eggs, etcetera, lots of bread. I brought it all down to my mum and my mum said "Where the hang did you get all that?" I says "These two soldiers". So she had to go out and meet these two guys.

They were really nice and asked about where we were staying. They realised then that we didn't have a place to stay. So they said "Well, I'll take you to a place. I know an old lady that'll take you in. We can only ask her," he says. I always remember his saying that. "We can only ask her," he says, "but I don't think she'll say no". So he took us right down the Granco, to the lane before Granco House.

We came in the lane there and there was this wee place, Granco Cottage, it was called, a heavenly place. We met Mrs. Hutton, a real nice old lady.

When I came back in later years and looked at where just one wall of the cottage still remains, it was small, but at our age it was huge. The cottage is gone, apparently the building went on fire.

Helen (Flannagan) Mann, Rothesay:
I was born the July twenty-third, 1936. I can't remember really much of Glasgow.

My first memories are of things here: of coming down the hill on the Lower Granco with my mother. I had a new pantaloon set on: pantaloons, a coat and a blue bonnet. They were swinging me between them, the soldier and my mum.

When we went into Mrs. Hutton's, there was a big fireplace, a great big grate. And in the other room, it looked to me an enormous bed. I suppose it was just a double bed. When we came in, there was a young boy on the bed. I don't know who he was, nor the woman who was also there. The little boy was playing with a spinning top. I was put on the bed beside him and I ended up taking the spinning top from him and I got into trouble for that, I'm afraid.

Helen (Flannagan) Mann

I remember Mrs. Hutton had a grandfather clock. She used to keep her sugar and all that in it. She used to bank all her rations in it so we couldn't get it…in case my mother stole anything from her.

Mrs. Hutton lived in the house with us. She stayed in the kitchen, and we stayed through in the other room, my mother, brother and I. I realise now it must have been very small, but I remember everything being so big, even the door. I'd have to bend down now going in that door.

There was one window looked on to the garden, I remember, because a cat came in one night when we were sleeping. Either the window was open or broken and the cat got in and we were screaming like anything. My brother yelled to get my mother through and she helped to get it out because we thought it was a rat or something with its eyes gleaming in the dark.

Jack Flannagan: Helen said that she remembers a cat coming into the bedroom. The window was small, small panes of glass, maybe nine or twelve small panes, but the one at the top opened. That was to let air in.

I can remember meeting Mrs. Hutton, small, plump, glasses, hair in a bun, and wearing a white apron. To a young lad she was a nice woman, she was good to us. She said "Aye, you can move in right away." She'd change the bed in the bedroom.

"Away up and get your stuff," she said. We went up and got our cases and things and brought them down. The two soldiers, they called one Corky, after Corky the cat in Beano, and the other one was called Sash. The two brought the stuff down for my mum and I. They saw us in, so they were friends from the very start.

There was a burn at the bottom of the street, and I caught my first fish in that burn. With a hook and a thread I caught it just under the gills. Poor wee thing, I put it back in again, I was broken-hearted, because I'd nearly stamped it to death. That was Dunning Burn.

Near where the Thorntree Inn is, there used to be a spare piece of ground, and there'd be old cars in there. That was an adventure to us, we had every different car to drive, nineteen twenty models and nineteen thirty models, all of them scrap of course. We played in there quite a bit.

I followed the burn down to where it meets the River Earn. We used to do that quite regularly. It's a real adventure because it's quite a walk from the village to follow the burn down. And we followed the Burn away up past the Dragon, nice waterfalls there. We used to go way up there, into really deep parts of it, where the water used to foam up.

And up there was the sand quarry, with all the sand martins. I think it was a sheer mistake the first time we came on the quarry. We went up past the Park and then we came across this quarry. I used to lie for hours on the edge of that quarry just watching these birds. I didn't know what the hell they were, to me they were swallows, because they had the sweptback wing. I
knew what a swallow was in those days.

Then somebody told me they were sand martins. By God, there were thousands of them, absolute thousands! I watched them for ages. I went to school one morning, and just went up that way and thought I'd look in on the birds. I never went to school. I don't think my mother was any the wiser either.

Helen Flannagan: We used to paddle in the burn and get fish out of there. We used to catch them with our stockings, our ankle socks. If you found a hole in the wall lining the burn you used to put your fingers in and maybe get a fish out. It didn't always work. Nine times out of ten it didn't but sometimes you put your sock over the hole and you got out a fish. When it rained the water from the burn used to come up to our door, and the ducks came up the street. My mother got a row for that too, for feeding them. Everyone complained.

There used to be an old man collecting sticks. He had a hook and used to get stuff out of the burn you know like bits of trees and things for the winter.

Yes, the burn used to come to the door of the cottage, along the alley. That was a saying my mother had. How much do you love me? Deep as the Dunning Burn. (laughs). Not so very deep most of the time now, is it?

Jack Flannagan: My dad used to come up weekends. He used to stand all the boys in the pub a drink and I think it was a Mr. Thompson in the pub, in The Thorntree. He always had whisky. My dad didn't know where the hell he got it but he always had whisky. My dad was a good whisky man. He used to buy all the lads a drink and they were very pleased to see him. They used to always say to me, when I'd be maybe walking up the street, "Is your bloody old man coming this week?" (laughs) "Yes, yes," I'd say.

Helen (Flannagan) Mann: My mother didn't like it much because of the guns, the artillery pieces, along the street. She thought we were still going to get the war here. Guns along the street and a garage for the army trucks just down the alley and she thought we're not too far away from the war.

She was scared that they were still going to get us here. But then she realised it wasn't dangerous. It was real quiet here.

We used to get tyres off the lorries from the soldiers. The boys used to cover them with all different colour of chalks and roll down the hills inside them, falling into the water, and getting into trouble for that as well.

The soldiers were all around. They used to come in quite a lot and have a cup of tea with my mother. I remember the soldiers used to go to the village hall for the dancing and we always sat on the stage and they used to give us drinks, orange and that. We used to get a glass of ginger or whatever was going during the war, and then afterwards we came home with our mothers.

I remember the very first day I started school. I was sitting there and my mother was standing at the door and the teacher gave me a tin---I can remember it was a Capstan cigarette tin---and it had rings in it. She gave me a board with nails on it and told me to count these rings on to the nails, and tell me how many rings were there. I kept looking up to see if my mother was there. Then when I looked up my mother had disappeared so I started screaming. So she said to me "Don't cry, because your brother's here as well." There was a sliding panel thing that separated the two classrooms and when she opened it I could see my brother sitting there in the classroom and I was all right then because I knew he was there. And that's about all I really remember about going to school in Dunning.

Remember other evacuees? Well I just thought we were the only ones here. I thought everyone else at school just sort of belonged here. I knew we were from Glasgow but I thought we were the only ones. Long afterwards I heard the term "Glasgow keelies"---maybe I heard it at the time but I didn't take any notice of it.

Did I ever get into trouble? Oh, I suppose I did but I shoved that to the back of my mind. I can't ever really remember getting into trouble. I mean my parents used to give me belts on the ear and things like that like everybody else but (laughs) I can't remember what the hell for, though at the time I must have. If you get a belt on the ear you must have deserved it somewhere along the line. I can't ever remember getting into trouble here. Except for staying off school, which I think everybody did. If you stayed off school they used to come look for you and find you and drag you back to the school. The School Board (was that what you called him?) used to drag you back to school.

I used to go anywhere, mostly the other side of the burn. There must have been places to hide over there because that's where we always went. I didn't like school. It was like a prison term to me. I was glad to be done with it in the end.

Jack Flannagan: Here it was dead easy to stay away from school, compared to Glasgow. Here they had an old guy who we called the School Board. I think he'd only the one leg. You can outpace a fellow with just one leg. Well at nine years of age you can outpace any bugger, you know. He would come round to the houses and tell your mother and father that you weren't in school such and such days You know, with Dad not being here, we didn't have that father control that we should have had.

Once I took a rabbit to school. I put it down the front of my trousers. The teacher asked "What have you got in there?" "Nothing, nothing." But the rabbit wanted out. It was a wild rabbit I'd adopted and it wanted out, and of course when a rabbit wants out, it just scratches. It tore all my stomach. Of course I let it out and it ran around the classroom and everybody was chasing it. Then, alas, I had to let it go.

Somebody told me that waterhens' eggs were good. I think one of the soldiers had told me if you ever see waterhens (I think they lay maybe eight or nine eggs) "If you break one, find them young, everything's fine. Leave them with maybe a couple, take the rest away, you know." First when I brought them home, my mum she wouldn't cook them. It was Mrs. Hutton who said they were very good. I think we boiled them.

Jack Flannagan

97

And they were lovely, absolutely beautiful.

Helen (Flannagan) Mann: There were hens in the garden next door. Every now and then the soldiers would get us hens from there. They used to climb over the washhouse roof and steal hens out of the garden behind and then bring them to us and we could have a chicken for dinner. I remember they brought one in one night and it wasn't dead. It was flying all over the place. They hadn't wrung its neck right or something.

Jack Flannagan: The soldiers used to go to steal the chickens but they had nobody to cook them for them. So my mum says I'll cook them for you if you're going to steal them. They went away down the burn to where there were a couple of henhouses. They asked me do I want to come. It was a big adventure that to a rogue like me. This guy took the chicken and wrenched its neck. That's all you do, he said. I thought "Ugh ". I took one by the legs and brought it home and put it on the table and the damn thing was alive. It flew all around the house. It was absolutely chaotic. Everyone panicked trying to catch that chicken. You just don't forget things like that: at nine years, everything's an adventure to you.

In summer, there are wasps all over the place. My mother was terrified of them. I got the job of swatting them. Helen and I got a small tin with six bees…we thought they were bees but they were wasps…and we closed the lid and we buried them outside the bedroom window. Helen says the kitchen window, but I say the bedroom window. We looked for it coming back, but the tin would have rotted by this time. It was an important burial for us.

When we were young Helen and I were very close. Especially when we were here in Dunning, Mother said Helen goes nowhere unless you're with her. Helen was along at the end of the lane. There was long grass and the sun had sort of browned it all. There were four guys picked on Helen. I come along and being the big brother I was called to sort these guys out. But there were four of them and I thought what the hell I'm not tackling four of them, you know, even for my sister. They hid in the long grass and they were shouting "Glasgow keelie, Glasgow keelie" to me. I was quite angry because I couldn't sort them out. so I came down to the house, took a box of matches and went up and set fire to the damn grass. (laughs) That soon shifted them. They ran like hell then, the grass was on fire.

I got into trouble for that, the police were down for that. I think there was only one policeman in Dunning at that time.

Was I in trouble a lot? Ahh, no, no, I daresay not. We did have some bother once about letting cows out on to the village. We went looking what we thought were fish on the other side of the burn. We put them in a shortbread tin, brought them home and put them in the washhouse. We didn't tell Mrs. Hutton or anybody because this was our secret. But they were tadpoles and I'm afraid their tails fell off and they were frogs the next day. The place was alive with frogs. My mother nearly died. She went out to do her wash in the washhouse and "The place is full of frogs!"

Ah, but the thing was when we came back from the other side of the burn, I'd left the gate lying open. And all these bullocks got out and they were all over the damn village. They were up on the main street. They'd just walked through the burn. We got into trouble for that. The police came again to see us about that and told my mother that she'd have to keep her children under control. But then again we were Glasgow keelies, and we got away with it. I think quite honestly that was why we got away with quite a lot, because we didn't know country life. It was a funny thing to us.

I think we were here about three years altogether. The day we left, the war was on the verge of finishing. My father phoned the grocer's shop. It was the only way he could get in touch with us. The lady came down from the shop and told us we were to go home. The damn war was finished, my father said, come home, he says.

We packed up everything, said cheerio to Mrs. Hutton and we went up and got on the bus.

Helen (Flannagan) Mann: Wee bits of memories come jogging into my mind. I loved it here, I really did. I'd come back, I would, if I could drag my husband along. I like it. I don't know, just something about it. (Wipes her eye) I'm getting a bit filled up now.

At the first Evacuees Reunion in Dunning, September 3, 1994,
George Boardman poses for photographers with a gas mask

German planes scout the Forth Bridge

Chapter 13: RELATIVE SAFETY

At various times during the war, and from various endangered parts of Britain, children were evacuated to the safety of Dunning relatives. Here are three stories of "unofficial" or "private" evacuees.

The first comes from brothers Jim Hepburn, now of Dunoon, and Don Hepburn, now of Scarborough, Ontario. They were born in Dunning, but when they were infants the family moved to Edinburgh.

James Hepburn, Dunoon: The fateful Sunday when war was declared we were actually in Dunning visiting our grandparents. My brother and I were evacuated to the village twice, the first time to our grandfather's in the village itself. The second time we were split between two aunts, he in the village and me to Boghall Farm, from where I walked to the village school every day.

Don Hepburn, Scarborough, Ontario: With the evacuation in full swing, Dunning was the place of choice for my brother John and me. As we had lots of relatives there, it was decided to separate us, probably so that we could charm a wider selection of relatives.

My best recollection of the following incident is that I was in transit in the family car between Edinburgh and Dunning. That places this event very early in the war, as petrol restrictions were imposed shortly after the war started and the car was then taken out of service for some time. Our usual route to cross the river Forth was via Kincardine Bridge. For some reason on this occasion we went via Queensferry.

We duly embarked on the ferry. About half way across, looking through the spans of the Forth Railway Bridge, we could see several aircraft heading our way, from the east. They were flying so low that one of them passed under the centre span of the bridge. As they continued over us they were identified as German, twin engine JU88 bombers. They then banked and turned back and proceeded to strafe the warships which were anchored in the river, off Rosyth. Eventually the warships, realising they had been caught napping, responded with a tremendous din.

In the meantime, our very exposed ferryboat sailed along, under this malevolent barrage, with occasional shrapnel landing on the deck. While the ruckus was deafening, I do not recall any injuries on the ferryboat or to the combatants. We could see damage to property on shore from the "friendly fire" of the warships, which were firing their big guns at the low flying aircraft. With this episode the war seemed very real and personal and afterwards, I was glad to be in the hidden refuge of Dunning

A private evacuee who came to Dunning later in the war, Wilf James lives now at Peyriac de Mer in the south of France.

Wilf James: I was born in the town of Asbestos, in the province of Quebec. on June twenty-fourth, 1927. My parents had emigrated to Canada from England.

My father was working as an engineer with the asbestos mine there. During blasting operations, my father was hit by a rock on the side of the head, and died within twenty-four hours. I had been conceived only three months earlier.

When I was born, my mother made arrangements to come back to England and settle in the region of Egham Staines, just southwest of what is now Heathrow Airport. We stayed there for a while, while my mother took various domestic jobs.

I went to the local school, where I did not get on very well at all. My mother had a step-grandfather in Dunning, Perthshire, and his wife had a son who asked my mother, in about February or March of 1940, if she would like to come up and look after her grandfather, and get away from what would develop into a hot bombing area in England. Those were the reasons we arrived in Scotland in March, 1940.

My great-grandfather's name was Thomas Matthews and he was in his late eighties. He lived in Wester Keltie on Keltie Estate, Dunning, where he was a gamekeeper. His stepson Bob lived a distance away also in Perthshire, he was about twenty-five or thirty.

Bob was a gamekeeper in his own right up at Amulree, on the road past the Sma' Glen. I only met him once or twice. He met us at Gleneagles Station when we got off. A week or two later he left to go to the army. He came home on leave once, and then, travelling from Africa to India, his boat was blown to bits and he died.

I was thirteen when we came to Wester Keltie. My mother got me into the school in Auchterarder. I got on the little bus which ran from Dunning to Auchterarder, which all the evacuees were on. I just went down to the end of the road and got on the bus with all the evacuees, which is why I was included with them, though technically I wasn't really an official evacuee. I considered myself partially an evacuee, because we had evacuated ourselves.

My step-great-grandfather was a very old man with a beard. He had a whisky or beery nose. He didn't drink much that I knew of, but it had puffed his nose up so that it looked…well…I suppose you could say grotesque. I liked him though he was very hard on me, very strict. Not a Bible-thumper, but he did read his Bible every morning.

I learned from him that nearly everything could be made or adapted from something round about. For example, you could make snares for rabbits, and mole traps. And he taught me the ways of wildlife, like where rabbits and pheasant would go or wouldn't go. Things like that.

During the war we had to go out on fox drives. The one who organised them was the local policeman. The people who took part were the farmers or the shepherds or the elderly gamekeepers who weren't called up.

The evacuees among others were called out to be beaters for the pheasant shoots for what was left of the gentry.

I was also called on to work in the gardens at Keltie. When the petrol ran out for the mower, we had to cut the grass with scythes. The gardener, who lived next door to us, was called Young. In those days they were all referred to by their surnames, never their given names. The people at the castle were the Bowes-Lyons, relatives of the Queen Mother.

Also in my days at Keltie, I was asked to help run the private generating plant. It was a Lister diesel. I did that after I came home from school at night, two or three nights a week, and then Saturday I would give it a thorough cleaning and top up the batteries. Also during my schooldays, I worked in the projector box at Auchterarder cinema. Somebody asked the headmaster if there was anyone knowledgeable enough who could help run the cinema. So I was coming home from school and then cycling back to Auchterarder often to run two houses of the cinema, one at six and the other at eight, and not getting back until half past ten.

I used to work at potato picking occasionally for the Neills at the neighbouring farm of Rossie. When it was too wet for the automatic digger to scoot the tatties out, I would drive a pair of horses on a plough to turn up the tatties from the drill.

Fitting in with all these things was the Air Training Corps. A lot of us joined that. It took us three evenings a week, plus most weekends. I was in the pipe band, which was called out to play for the Wings for Victory campaigns, collecting scrap metal and anything else for the war effort. I played the pipes. We had to buy our own instruments. Born in Quebec, raised in England, and then became a piper in a Scots band!

I went to the wireless college in Dundee and took what they called a PMG certificate which was for going to sea. This was in early '44. By then they were sinking boats so fast, there were no positions for wireless operators. So, thanks to my ATC training, I joined the RAF.

John Dunn: I was born March 1, 1934 in a place in Surrey called Worcester Park. I just had one sister, who was about two years older than me.

My father was born in the Dunning area. Later he was a plumber in the village after my grandparents moved here from Auchterarder. My grandfather was a plumber too.

I'd already been to Scotland before the war, when I was about three. And I stayed with my gran above the plumbing shop in Dunning, on Auchterarder Road.

When war broke out we were living about twenty miles south of London. There were lots of air raids and bombings. We'd be in school, there'd be air raids, and we would have to go to the shelters. We had gas masks.

I used to enjoy the raids. We had no fear. The parents were frightened, but I was never frightened. I used to watch the guns blazing, and there was a lot of ack ack. There were barrage balloons, to catch the enemy planes

Jerry would drop a lot of bombs on London. Sometimes he had some bombs left and he'd drop them on the way back and they were just dropped anywhere. We all had shelters. Dad

John Dunn in Dunning

dug a big hole in the garden for an Anderson shelter, made of corrugated iron and earth and sandbags, with bunks inside. There were steps down into it. It was a clay bottom and used to fill up with water whenever it rained. Dad rigged up a hand pump and one of my jobs when I came home from school was to pump the water out of the bottom of the shelter. I was about seven at the time.

We had a big bomb land about six houses down on the opposite side of the road, a delayed action bomb. So everybody on the whole street had to get out. They were semi-detached houses and the bomb went down between two of them. Nobody was killed, lucky enough. But they cordoned off the street, about half a mile long. It took about two weeks before they cleared all that up, and meantime we'd had to move to relatives at Croydon.

Another incident I remember was that I broke my arm, and mum had to take me to the hospital. I had it set, came out and had to go back a week later. They X-rayed it, and they'd set it wrong. So they had to break it again. I hated gas, I was always ill if I had my teeth done with gas---the smell, you know. They gave me gas to reset my arm, and I was sick and I felt really bad. The doctor said I could stay in overnight.

It was Nelson Hospital, in south Wimbledon. That night the air raid warnings went, and there were guns going and the windows were rattling in the hospital. It was a real schamozzle, all the ack ack guns were trying to shoot down the planes. All of a sudden there's water coming through the ceilings and firemen are running in shouting "Everybody's got to get out!" They moved us into big houses across the road.

The hospital was on fire. They'd dropped about a hundred incendiaries on it. When we came out the whole roof was ablaze. All the firemen were up there. The guns were still going. We must have been in the houses an hour or so, and then the wardens knocked on the door. "Everybody out, you've got to get out." They had sent single-decker buses. Everything was in blackout, all the windows were blacked out. I remember lying on a seat in the bus. They drove around to different hospitals finding room to drop people off. I was in the bus for two or three hours.

I've forgotten which hospital I ended up in. The insurance man…they always came round the houses and collected the money every week…he happened to call on mum the morning after the raid and he said "Did you hear about the Nelson Hospital getting bombed last night? Incendiaries on it, it was all ablaze and there was one person killed." Of course mum thought it was me. It was a fireman who was killed when he fell off the roof. It took my mum about a week searching around the different hospitals before she found me.

The flying bombs started coming over at the beginning of the summer in 1944. The neighbour who lived next door to us, she had three children, her husband was away in the army. Her friend was at the bottom of the garden, she had two children, and they used to take turn about staying in each other's shelter each night for company. It was the turn of the lady next door to stay with her friend and they were all in the shelter. The mother happened to go to the outside toilet. A bomb came over, and I'll never forget it because I thought it was for us. The flying bomb comes over, the motor cuts out, and then they could glide for five miles or maybe drop like a stone. This one seemed like it was right over us, and it cut out.

We were in the Morrison shelter inside, which is like a big metal box. It was placed underneath the window so if a blast came the glass went into the other wall. The siren had already gone, but mum was out in the kitchen making a cup of tea or something. She dived in on top of us, and I can remember saying to her "I think this is our lot". There was this almighty crash, all the ceilings came down, the back door blew off and all the lino. There were fifteen killed, and the lady next door lost her three children and her friend and her two children. If it had landed a hundred yards shorter, I wouldn't be here today to tell the story.

It was decided things were getting too dangerous. All the other kids were getting evacuated, because there were a lot of houses bombed. I think a helluva lot of kids around my area got evacuated to different parts of the country, wherever anybody could take anybody in. My mother brought my sister and me up to Dunning to my grandparents.

I went to the school up the hill. I don't know how long I was there and I can't remember the teacher. But I know Mrs. Crow used to do the cooking in the school and I liked her rice pudding. If the skin was brown, I used to like it and a lot of kids didn't. The more cooked it was the browner it was, and I can remember going asking for more and getting nearly all the skin.

Then I went to the other school. The kids I can remember from the school were Dunning kids. The evacuees, a lot of them came from Glasgow, and one or two of them didn't like me because I was from London. I didn't have any problems with the local kids but some of the Glasgow kids were rough, and I got bullied a bit when I first came here.

There was a teacher called Miss Robertson. I remember her, and getting strapped by her once. It's a full strap, supposed to be just on the hand, but the strap caught me up here and I had two big welts on my wrist. I was never that naughty, just got the strap once, but it must have been something.

When I was at school, you had to learn poetry. One of the poems was "To a Mouse", by Burns. I was the first kid in the class to learn it, despite my being from London and all the other kids from Scotland. My grandfather taught me how to pronounce all the words. He used to go over and over them. The teachers were amazed that a Londoner could learn so well, but I really liked poetry.

I loved it in Dunning, especially the freedom. We used to go sledging up at the Park and down the Lower Granco. Sometimes when it was really icy, we used to go up the road to the wee school, and sledge down the road as fast as we could.

For the school I remember that we used to collect rose hips along the hedgerows. I think they went to Dr. Barnardo's, and they made rose-hip syrup. We used to get ha'penny a pound or something like that.

And we used to chase the girls. I don't know whether you've ever had a rose-hip broken open and put down your back, but it itches. We used to put them down the girls' necks sometimes.

There was no golf course then. It was all beautiful forest, right up to Maggie Walls' monument. Duncrub House, that's all pulled down now was still there then, majestic in the distance.

My grandad took me birdnesting. He showed me how to collect birds' eggs and to always make sure you only took one egg of each species. I had quite a collection of birds' eggs.

We used to go rabbiting as well, all the kids. We'd follow the combine harvester for the last 50 or so feet and all the rabbits would come out and we'd dive and catch them. We learned how to kill them, grabbing them by the back leg and breaking their neck over your shoe. Taking them home my grandfather would show me how to skin them and my gran would make rabbit pie.

Sundays were memorable. My grandad never went to church, but my gran was a churchgoer. As a result Sundays she would never cook a roast, there was no playing of cards, and she would not knit. There was nothing to do but to go to Sunday school or church, or walking. I was fortunate that my grandad would take me birdnesting, or a fellow across the road, Mr. Mitchell, would take me and show me how to guddle trout in Keltie Burn. Whether I was guddling or birdnesting, I was in my best clothes all Sunday.

I can remember being here for VE-day. We had a big bonfire. All the farmers cut fir trees and collected all the rubbish in the village. It was in the Park up the Dunnock where we set up the bonfire. It was a massive pile. Before lighting it, there was a dance in the Dunning Hall. Part way through, somebody came in and said a couple of local drunks had set fire to the bonfire. So everybody had to come out of the Hall and go up there, otherwise there wouldn't have been much left. I remember that, but who set it afire, I don't know.

For VJ Day I was at a street party in my old street in Surrey. I had cried my eyes out when I went back from Dunning, I didn't want to go home. I wanted to be back up here with my gran and grandad. I was a Scot then, my mum and dad could hardly understand what I was saying.

I finished school and eventually got a job as a lathe operator. One of my uncles came back from New Zealand with slides. I love trout fishing, and there's wonderful trout fishing in New Zealand, you can go anywhere, nobody owns river banks and fishing rights like here. My uncle offered to sponsor me, so, since we were just scratching out a living, my wife and I decided to emigrate and we went on assisted passage. And we've had no regrets.

But the time in Dunning was the happiest time of my life.

Guddling in the Dunning Burn: a pastime going back many generations

Chapter 14: HOLE IN THE HEART

***Mrs. Nita Pryde was born Nita Inglis in Glasgow in March, 1930.
Dunning was her eventual destination as an evacuee, and she recalled
her first year in Dunning as the freest of her life.***

Nita (Inglis) Pryde: When I was small, my friend Margaret had a big sister who
was at school, and we used to go around to the school all the time to see her. The
result was that they said "Oh, for goodness sake, just come to school!" with the
result that we started school when we were four and a half. It was a very good
school, Balornock in the north of Glasgow. I was about nine when war started so
I had been at that school all the time. I was an only child.

On September 3, I was evacuated with the school to Aberdeenshire, with my
mother going as a helper. We were billeted to a little croft, and it was lovely. But
I had an uncle and aunt, he was a minister in Aberdeen, and they came to see us
and said we couldn't stay there. It was just a croft, you see, and this Jeanie who
ran the croft had been expecting two boys who could help her in the croft, and
mother and I had arrived instead of two boys. So she wasn't geared up, she had
palliasses up in the attic for boys. We were very happy there, but we left after two
or three months.

Uncle David found us this beautiful estate on Deeside, just outside Aberdeen. It
was the home of two spinster sisters of a famous industrial family. They were very
mean, the old ladies, and martinets. We were all lined up at 7 o'clock for prayers.
They had a beautiful grand piano and my mother asked if I could practise, because
I was taking music at that time. "Oh, no." My cousin Calbert cycled from
Aberdeen to visit us. He was told to go round and come in the back way. They
were like that.

It was a beautiful house, and we had a fine room upstairs. I used to wake up in the
middle of the night hungry. We weren't getting enough food. They sent me off to
school. It was a wonderful walk through fields and over stiles and a lovely little
school in the middle of a pine wood. I had for my lunch a slice of white bread with
apple jelly, turned over and made into a sandwich, and a little syrup of figs bottle
with milk. That was it, that was my lunch. The headmaster and his wife had me
in and gave me soup to keep me going. When I went back at night, they served at
dinner all the lovely game things, partridge and pheasant, but we got only this
very small portion.

Nita Inglis

I was a growing child and I had a health problem, I had a hole in the heart. My parents didn't know until I was about seven. When I was having a bath I turned blue. They sent for the doctor, and he diagnosed the hole in the heart. There was nothing at that time you could do. So it was just a case of I wasn't allowed to do all sorts of things. I led a very restricted life. When everybody else got roller skates, I didn't, and when everybody got a bike, I didn't. I had to come back from school, go to bed, have a rest. So I had a really restricted, sheltered life.

My mother told the sisters, "Well, she's waking up in the middle of the night, and she's hungry." So I got a rich tea biscuit and a glass of milk for my supper. They were so mean, it was dreadful. It was such a beautiful house, and they were the spinster members of this very rich family.

One day I came back from school and my mother was all packed up. "We're going home." The servants, the cook and maybe three others had walked out. The sisters asked mother if she would cook and keep the place going until they got new servants. My mother's job had been just to answer the telephone and to get down on her hands and knees and do the morning room carpet.

Off we went to Glasgow, just in time for the Clydebank blitz. So we were evacuated for the second time. Six of us from Balornock School were billeted with Lady Wilson in beautiful Kippen House above Dunning. This time mother was not there. She had to let me go on my own. I would be about ten.

The girl I was most friendly with was Betty Fabian. Her brother John was billeted somewhere else in Dunning. The other girls were Ina Fairley, two sisters Ruby and Grace Fletcher and their cousin Ruth. I can't remember anyone else from our school who came to Dunning.

Lady Wilson's house was big and absolutely wonderful. When I visit National Trust property there is this certain smell and I am immediately transported back in time to Kippen House.

There was the main door and this other door leading into what was the ballroom. We had the ballroom. At our age, it seemed enormous. At one end there was a single bed, a huge made-up bed that took the three girls, and then Betty Fabian and I in a double bed. At the other end was the bed of the lady who looked after us, a Mrs. Colville from the village. Then there was the door out of the ballroom into a very wide corridor. Off the corridor was a door leading to the bathroom, with a big sunken bath, which we had a great time in. Then the toilet off that. Lady Wilson had put a partition with what they called a "bowlie"…this was all new to me, and it's an expression I've never heard since either…it was like a trap door in this partition and this is where our food was sent through. She had a cook and servants. She was a lovely old lady. Lady Wilson didn't have much to do with us, but when we arrived at first she had a chat with us. She must have lived in France at one time as she taught us how to curtsy to her when we met her "as the little French girls did".

There was a summer-house outside, a moveable one you could push on its axis, like a roundabout. It rotated obviously to catch the sun, but we belted it around. There was a beautiful room with window seats all around the bottom of this huge window. They were filled with books for children, wonderful books. I had a wonderful time up there. Not having mother with me, I went wild, having had this very restricted life. I was away running and climbing trees and going up the hill and…it was just wonderful. Absolutely blissful.

It was quite a long walk to school—my school in Glasgow had been just around the corner from my house.

We soon discovered a shortcut to the school—across the river—two wires, one to stand on and the other above to hold onto. It was a tremendous shortcut for us, and then we had a long walk uphill back to Kippen House, really long when it was wet, but my hole in the heart didn't seem to hinder me. I had a new lease of life!

The evacuees did not go to the village school. We were taught by a Glasgow teacher in what had been the cookery and woodworking class. We had this wonderful teacher from Haghill School, and her name was Miss Haggart. Her nickname was Haggybags, but she was a terrific teacher.

I take my hat off to this teacher. She had five to eleven year olds in the one room. That woman had to teach everyone, infants up to sub-qualifying, age five to ten, in separate groups in the one classroom. When we older pupils had finished our work we helped with the younger ones. She must have been exhausted. And she had to be a bit of a martinet because there were some real rough boys, wild.

When I was staying at Kippen, in the middle of the day for lunch we had to go in to Belle Flockhart's shop. We went in there and had a roll and margarine, a bottle of school milk, and a Paris bun. (I've never been able to look at a Paris bun since. It's just a plain bun with little sugar lumps across the top, that's all.)

Back to Kippen after school, we lived, ate and slept in the ballroom. The food for our evening meal was very good and we were always ready for it!

We roamed all over the hills and guddled for fish in the burn and altogether had a wonderful time. We seemed to be completely removed from the war. But, as time wore on, not that long, everybody else began to get homesick… and weepy. When it came time for the mothers to visit the children would cry and want to go home. Not me! But they all eventually went. I didn't want to go, because I was having a ball.

My mother and aunt decided that they would get a small place in the village to rent in the Commercial Buildings, West End, Dunning. So instead of going home to Glasgow, I went down to the village. There was my aunt Peggy, with her two children. I would be about ten, Lloyd would be about six, Marian would be about three.

Two and a half years I was there in Dunning in all, Kippen House and the Commercial Buildings. It's such a part of me. It was so different from Glasgow. There was one year when the snow was right up to the top of the hedges on the way down to the Broom. We were just cut off: a different life altogether.

We then went down to sit our qualifying at the Dunning School, with a Mr. Benzies, who was the headmaster.

I seemed to blossom in Dunning, and I guess the doctors figured I couldn't be that badly off. My mother was busy, she'd taken a wee job across in the baker's, Robertson's. When we were down in the village, I became friendly with a family who were evacuated from England, and she had a horse. Diana Sorrel was my friend's name. I rode the horse, and I rode a bike, and I just had a ball. I think this is the reason why Dunning means so much to me, because it was the place I had my freedom.

The soldiers were billeted all about, Poles and others. They were just part of life, they had their films in the village hall, just across from where we stayed in the Commercial Buildings. You got a soldier to take you in, and you sat with other children way up on the window sills.

The local and evacuee kids seemed to integrate. But you were mostly friends with other evacuees. I did have a friend Leila Mailer, who lived on a farm near the village. I used to go up there to play. I used to run up into the loft where the hay was and jump down…it was "Keep the Pot Boiling". And one of our jobs was to go round and right the sheep. You know when they fall on their backs they can't get up again. Leila and I had to go round and haul them up.

There were hazel bushes way up the hill and there was an estate out the Bridge of Earn Road with a walnut tree. We knew where all the fruit trees were in people's gardens. There was Miss Watt and she had fruit trees. And the garage had a pear tree. One day the police came into the school, into the classroom, and wanted to know who had been raiding the gardens. Of course, we were all at it. I think the whole lot of us came forward.

We used to play this "Tick Tack". I used to be just a hanger-on at "Tick Tack". It was like a bobbin with a nail and somehow they would fix it on a window. Then there was a thread leading round the corner. It was the boys of course who pulled it. It tapped on the window. And then you just ran for your life when the door opened. Dearie me, we just had a wonderful time.

To me it was a completely new world from being closeted and cosseted, taken care of, you mustn't do this or that.

Here I just had the time of my life. I fell into the burn too, in winter. We were going across the wires over the burn just for fun. Of course, in the middle it's quite deep. I was wearing a kilt, and you know how much material they have, and a Harris tweed coat, and long stockings that mother had knitted. I fell into the water. Then I had to get myself through the village. Everything was so heavy I could hardly stand up straight.

I won a bursary to Perth Academy after the qualifying. My parents debated this and decided no. They wouldn't let me go to Perth Academy, because it meant a long walk to the Broom to catch the train, and there seemed to be all kinds of shenanigans went on in this train. You got to Perth then you had another walk or bus. This of course was, again, the consideration of…the hole in the heart.

I ended up going to Auchterarder. It was a junior secondary, and I had to take a commercial course. I was a whole year and a half at Auchterarder, before going back to Glasgow. When I got back to the secondary school in Glasgow, I didn't want commercial. I always wanted to be a teacher, and it was a struggle but I got there in the end.

Then, I might not be able to be a teacher because of…the hole in the heart. It followed me everywhere. I had to go to the Royal Infirmary in Glasgow, and be x-rayed in great detail, and another doctor connected with the teacher training college examined me all upside down and roundabout. It was all to do with the superannuation, the teachers' pension scheme.

Then came the great day I was told, yes, I could be a teacher. I went to Jordan Hill College to study to be a teacher. The English teacher wanted me to go to university and get an M.A. but again they thought it would be too much for me with the hole in the heart. My heart didn't bother me, after I'd been in Dunning. Mind you in secondary school I wasn't allowed to take gym and things like that.

Was all the sheltering necessary? Yes, because when my heart problem did begin to show was when I got married and had my first child. My husband was a very open-air type and we used to camp and hillwalk.

When I had my first child they asked me if I would have this operation. It was still a deep-freeze method they used, to repair the hole in the heart. But I said no, I'm not bad, so they let that go. Then I had a second baby, and while I was carrying Les, I would be stirring the porridge and I would suddenly faint. Standing in a queue at a van, I would suddenly crumple. So it was beginning to show then. I had the second baby, it was also a Rhesus Negative. And the doctor came and said "Well, you've no option. You have to have this operation, if you want to look after your family." That's when he gave me ten years to live, at most, if I didn't have it.

By this time, they were using a heart and lung machine for this operation, and so I was one of the first to have this operation with the machine. So they repaired the hole in the heart. I took a long time to recover. I was thirty-one.

I had an interesting career as a teacher, but when my husband fell ill, I took early retirement at age 54.

How is my heart now? Fine. There's nothing wrong with the repair to the heart. It's the lungs which were affected all those 31 years before I had the operation. The blood kicking back into the lungs damaged them, and as I'm getting older, the elasticity is going out of the body, and this is what is scuppering me now.

The experience in Dunning was tremendous. It gave me this love of the countryside. I would have gone and stayed in Dunning but of course that's not the way things worked out. But it was a wonderful experience.

Mrs. Nita Pryde died on February 19/99,
apparently from complications arising from diverticulitis.

September 18, 1940. The passenger liner
"City of Benares" is sunk in the North Atlantic

About Other Evacuations

Chapter 15: MISSING THE BOAT

On September 3, 1994, former World War II evacuees to Dunning attended a fifty-five year evacuees reunion, part of which involved visiting local area schools to talk to pupils. Mrs. Jill Mitchell was then head teacher at Aberuthven School near Dunning. Among the visitors to her class that day were Dunning evacuee Mrs. Marion (Inglis) Leah and her husband Bud. Meeting for the first time, Mrs. Mitchell and Mr. Leah discovered that in 1940 each of them had been scheduled to go to Canada as evacuees, and both were booked to leave on the same ship, the City of Benares. For different reasons they each missed the sailing.

Bud Leah, Leeds: My name is Harry Leah. I was born in Manchester in 1928. I got the nickname Bud from an uncle of mine who emigrated to America, a bit of a gangster who came back to visit once and nicknamed me Bud, and it's stuck ever since.

When war broke out, I was not evacuated: my parents decided against it. Then, when the blitz on Manchester started around Christmas 1940, I was evacuated with many others, mostly to Lancashire seaside places. I was sent away to St.

Anne's, and I was there three or four months. When we got there…typical British organisation…nobody knew we were coming. They had to book us into the local community hall. There were about twenty or thirty of us sleeping on camp beds, on the stage of the community hall. This was also used as a drill hall, so during the evenings, we were able to watch the local defense volunteers doing their training.

After two or three weeks, they managed to billet us, mostly with the landladies on the seafront. We were billeted until March or April, and I think the reason I came home was that the landladies wanted the rooms for the Spring visitors. Even in war there must have been trippers to the seaside. The school was a sort of extension to the church, like a church hall, and the teachers were a couple of older fellows. The younger ones had been called away to the army.

The main trouble was that being at the seaside, you didn't feel like going to school, and you played truant. One of the things they used to do to stop us playing truant was to make us write an essay on what we did that particular afternoon when we played truant. After we had to re-write it and re-write it and re-write it, till we were sick to flaming death of writing these damn essays. But it used to stop us playing truant because you used to say God you'd have to write another essay! (laughs)

I was thirteen and I came back to Manchester because my Dad went on night work and my mum being deaf couldn't hear the sirens.

One of my mother's uncles had emigrated to Canada in the twenties. He'd bought or been granted some land in North Battleford, Saskatchewan. He then came to England in 1937 because his mother was ill and he came to look after his interests. Because his father had been quite rich he lived basically the life of a gentleman until about 1939, looking after his mother. He was under the impression she was on her last legs and about to die and leave him all the money. She lived about thirty years after him. She lived to be something like 95.

He had Canadian nationality, and when war broke out he was eligible to go back to Canada. That's when he suggested that I should go with him. Various papers had to be signed about custody. He couldn't just take me out of the country willy-nilly, not being a direct relation. Then we had signed all the papers and everything had been sorted out.

We were supposed to meet the ship in Liverpool. But for some reason, which I'm not really sure of…he'd been gored by a bull on his farm and his eyesight wasn't very good…I've some idea that they had written to him and told him when and where to meet the ship. I don't think he appreciated what the letter was, and he'd put it to one side. So we never actually got to the ship. We missed it.

That ship was the City of Benares, bound for Canada with evacuee children and others and was torpedoed with great loss of life. That stopped evacuees going to Canada. After the war, I became a marine engineer and sailed for eight years. It was then I was able to figure out that the ship I had missed as a child was the evacuee ship that had been sunk.

In September 1994, when we had the Dunning evacuees' reunion, all the visitors went out to speak at neighbouring schools. My wife and I and others went to speak to the primary pupils at nearby Aberuthven School. It turned out the headmistress at Aberuthven had lived in London at the time war broke out, and she was supposed to meet that ship to go to Canada and for some reason she didn't arrive there. It was an amazing coincidence: we both had had a similar escape, and here we were, many years later, crossing paths for the first time at a little Scottish school.

Harry 'Bud' Leah

Jill (Richards) Mitchell, Aberdalgie: My sister and I were born in south London, in Mitcham. I remember going to school in August 1939, just five and starting school.

We didn't know what war meant, but we understood we would soon have to go away. That was before the bombing, before there was any sign of war. This was the silent period, the "phoney war" up to 1940 and then came the aerial Battle of Britain.

During the Battle of Britain, we had an Anderson shelter in the garden and we must have lived in it for some weeks.

I can see it clearly even now: my mother had to go from the shelter to get something. It was just along the back of the house. She ran and I was at the shelter door and I screamed at her "Come back, come back!" And there was shrapnel coming down, showering down. Incredible, you know, and people lived through that. We weren't bad, we were south London, we weren't middle London and we weren't near the docks.

It was decided that we would be evacuated. This was a personal thing my parents decided. By this time my father was back in the R.A.F. He'd been in the First War. He was stationed in the Admiralty first of all, he was too old for active service. And then he was sent to Bletchley Park, "Station X", the code-breaking centre.

It was decided that we should be evacuated out of London. My parents decided we would go to Canada. They reckoned it was the safest place, I don't know why. Whether that was because of propaganda, I don't know.

So we were booked on the City of Benares, sailing from Liverpool in September, 1940. It was safer to go from Liverpool than London at that time.

At the last minute, or so the story goes now, my mother decided that she couldn't bear us to leave, to go so far away, so she cancelled the booking. My mother and sister and I went to Tring to stay with my mother's great-aunt. Tring is only thirty miles from London, but it was considered safer than staying in London. We were much luckier than most evacuees, my mother was with us, and we knew where we were going, to a relation.

It's always been in the back of my mind, that I just missed going to Canada on the City of Benares. When we had the evacuees' reunion in 1994, some people who had been evacuees to Dunning came to speak to the pupils at our school in Aberuthven, close by.

The evacuees were telling of their World War II experiences to the children and one of them, Bud Leah, mentioned The City of Benares. And suddenly the memory came back to me, of how my sister and I had been booked to go on that ship and my mother decided at the last minute to keep us with her.

Mrs. Jill (Richards) Mitchell

I guess we had known at the time that the City of Benares had been sunk, but it didn't register. "Oh, that boat went down". I don't think it meant anything to us. Nothing had happened to us and here we were in Tring and everything was great. And I never talked to anyone about our having been booked on that boat.

But when Bud Leah mentioned it, I felt a real shock.

Because I realised that had we been on that boat, I wouldn't be here now, I wouldn't have had all these years of life. Or had my sister and I been among the survivors, we would have had the horrible trauma of the experience to get over. An experience far worse than just being taken away from our parents.

Thinking about the whole evacuation scheme, obviously the aim was to save the children, to take them away to a safe place and if things worked out they could come back later, but they would at least be alive, the future generations. But I can't think it was a terribly good idea for the number of children who were affected, though it was a very small proportion of the population, wasn't it? But for those affected it must have been very traumatic, leaving a scar. Some of them may look back with gratitude, they were happy, they had a nice comfortable home, they were well looked after. But some were not so fortunate, treated like slaves perhaps, some of the farms I think misused the children as free labour. Everybody has their own story, obviously, of how they were treated.

Footnote: What happened to the City of Benares:

Captain Landles Nicholl was captain of the City of Benares and commodore of an unprotected convoy. His 11,000 ton passenger liner was torpedoed on 18th September, 1940, by U48 under Captain Heinrich Bleichrodt some 600 miles west of Ireland beyond the range of British navy escorts at this time. Few lifeboats were launched because the ship went down quickly.

There were about 400 passengers, including some 90 children being sent to Canada under the Children's Overseas Resettlement Scheme. About 300 passengers were lost, including 77 of the children. The remaining 100 survivors, passengers and crew, including 13 children, were spotted by an aircraft a week later and rescued by destroyers.

A Dutch liner, the Volendam, had been damaged by a torpedo but not sunk on 30th August, 1940, with 321 children on board. All were saved. After these incidents and the subsequent bad publicity the Resettlement Scheme was suspended. The Germans had declared unrestricted submarine warfare around Britain on 17th August, 1940, so the risks were known.

The media at the first Evacuees Reunion, Dunning,
September 3, 1994

Chapter 16: EVACUEES ELSEWHERE

While we were collecting the memoirs of evacuees coming to Dunning, we became aware of other interesting evacuee stories connected to the village. These were the stories of people now living in Dunning whose experiences happened elsewhere in Scotland. Here are the stories of three such people.

a. A Peaceful War

Written by Finella Lendrum, now Mrs. Wilson of Newton of Pitcairns, Dunning

Lesley and Finella Lendrum, Inverary,1940

Two little girls stood quietly looking through the hedge which separated their grandmother's house from the house next door. The year was 1943 and the house next door had been made the headquarters of the Western Coastal Command. Suddenly the children dissolved into giggles as they watched the military band who were playing on the lawn for the entertainment of King George VI, in Inverary on an official visit. It had probably never occurred to the powers that were, that the band would have to fend off an attack during their performance. My sister and I, although amused by the spectacle, also felt some sympathy for the men who were attempting to play while frantically swatting their faces and desperately trying to keep the clouds of vicious Argyllshire midges at bay.

Life for two children evacuated from possible wartime dangers in Glasgow to peaceful Loch Fyneside was actually full of wartime excitement. Next door to where we were staying with our grandmother was Admiralty House, with its signal man installed in a little look-out tower, flashing messages out over the loch. Behind the house stood extensive naval and military camps occupied by British, Canadian, Polish and Russian troops. Anchored in the loch were rows of tank landing craft, destroyers and a hospital ship distinguished by the huge red cross painted on its side.

Beside the front gate of granny's garden, occupying a small lock-up garage was an anti-aircraft gun. Somehow its presence did not appear very menacing amid the almost domestic atmosphere. It was heightened by our stout little housekeeper who bustled down every evening with a tray of tea and scones for the grateful gunner.

We were too young to realise what unusual circumstances these were, or in what strange surrounding we lived. We accepted the fact that in an odd way we were witnessing part of the war, but for us a war without combat or bombs. We also took it for granted that the peaceful waters of Loch Fyne were disturbed by a fleet of ships and its shores littered with troops, tanks and camps. The only time we really experienced something of the war was the night that Clydebank was blitzed. In the dark, the sky over the mountains around Loch Fyne glowed red.

Every aspect of our life was coloured by the war, but there was no feeling of danger or threat to our safety as small girls. I have no recollection of being warned not to speak to strangers and had a kind of freedom which would be unthinkable today. We walked to school and were whistled at by columns of soldiers marching past. We returned along the fine old avenue at the back of the town and learned to recognise the different types of tanks, one parked between each pair of the ancient beech trees planted by a Duke of Argyll.

An officer's pass for the army cinema was acquired through a friend, and every week we trotted off to the pictures, once and sometimes twice. We always tried to arrive early in order to find a place in the front row as the floor was completely flat. The chairs were hard folding seats set out on the concrete base of a huge Nissen hut, but we never noticed the discomfort. No doubt the films were hardly suitable for our tender years, but I was always entranced and would come out at the end in a dream, imagining myself as one of the screen actresses taking part in a real live drama. This euphoric state carried over into our walk home, trudging through the dark with our torches.

Immediately behind our garden was a camp occupied by Polish soldiers. They chatted through the hedge in their very limited English and tried to teach us some Polish words. The only ones I can still remember are good morning and monkey. I think the latter was a description of our behaviour as we were keen tree climbers. The Poles always seemed very handsome and concerned about their appearance. We were told that some of them wore hairnets to keep their hair in place at night.

One day we encountered a young American sailor sitting—we thought rather boldly—on the wall at the bottom of the garden. He was very puzzled about the existence of the wall and wanted to know why it was there and what it was for. He told us that he came from Texas and had never seen a wall round a garden in his whole life.

Two English sailors from neighbouring Admiralty House became adopted members of our household and took the role of wartime uncles to us. In the evening our daytime playroom turned into a place of relaxation for them, and they used to play chess and listen to music on our old wind up gramophone. One of them spent much of his leisure drawing and painting and became a fairly well known artist who later had an exhibition in Paris. We remember him as the young sailor with his white collar and bell bottoms, and were delighted that we still have two pen and ink sketches he made of our playroom. Every so often our two friends disappeared for long periods and came back with bristling beards, teasing us by giving us prickly kisses. I never asked them where they had been and only realised years later that they must have been away on active service. It also occurred to me that they must have been very young themselves, nineteen or twenty years old. Having this home from home in our grandmother's house must have meant a great deal to them.

Because of its important naval headquarters Inverary was visited by several leading wartime figures. When the King arrived on that warm and midgy summer day, he got out of his car at the gate of Admiralty House, smiling and waving at the little group which had gathered. We sat on the corner of granny's wall and waved back at the small figure in naval uniform.

We knew he was the King, but on this occasion he simply seemed part of the scene we had become used to. King Haakon of Norway and Winant, the U.S. Secretary of State we also saw arriving next door. The two visitors I remember most vividly, I suppose because even to a young child they were the best known and revered of all, were Churchill and Montgomery.

Our two years of evacuation came to an end and we returned to the city. What we had experienced was an unusual side of World War II. We lived in the midst of guns, tanks and warships, but I do not think that I connected those with what I vaguely knew was going on elsewhere.

b. Character-forming

Ron Thow's family has long connections with Dunning, where he now lives in Newton of Pitcairns.

In 1939 I would have been ten years old, an only child, living in Edinburgh. When the war broke out my father was keen that I should get away. He'd been in the infantry in the '14-18 war, and I think he knew what was coming. And so I was evacuated privately. He made the arrangements himself. After a couple of attempts, I finished up spending probably about two years in Callander.

At first I was sent down to stay with a family cousin in the Borders, but she was elderly and it was understood that I couldn't stay with her long. It was a rather remote valley near Selkirk, and it was very pleasant. I was very happy there.

From there I went to an Edinburgh School called John Watson's, and they moved the entire school down to Marchmount House, a stately home in Berwickshire. I stayed there a year but I wasn't particularly happy there.

Then came Callander, which was a very happy experience. I was in several homes there. I think my father had a friend in Callander and that was the contact, though I didn't actually stay with them.

The first place in Callander wasn't successful. It was a pretty curious household. I thought she was an old lady, but she was probably just middle-aged. She bred dogs, and had about fifteen of them. She lived in a cottage well out of town. By this time I was used to being away from home. But it was a dirty place, not much housekeeping done. She was an eccentric old lady. I was there just two weeks.

My family just took one look at this, and I was glad to get away: it was away out of town and there was no company. There were other evacuees there but they all disappeared quickly too.

I then went to a household where they had a daughter about my age. By this time I was eleven. That was fine for a while. It was in the town and I was very happy. I was there maybe six months.

Then I went to a very nice retired woman, I think she had been an art teacher. She also had one of the masters from the school as a boarder. He was called up by the air force shortly after I arrived. And that was fine. It was all very educative. You were open to new influences. And it was a good school, the McLaren School, the high school for the area.

There was a scout troop which gave the likes of us who weren't townspeople, a focal point in the evenings. We'd go off and have campfires and this sort of stuff on the weekends. There was no scoutmaster, it was just run by one of the senior boys. It wasn't a highly disciplined troop.

There was very much a sense of being at war. Callander was full of the army, regiments coming and going all the time. The woods around were full of ammunition dumps and firing ranges.

We were aware of the Clydeside blitz in Callander. I had a west-facing attic window. We could hear the noise of the bombs, and see the flames on two or three nights. We could hear planes. One plane, I think a British fighter, crashed on Ben Ledi and we could see the flames. And then the next day, all the Glasgow kids came, looking very shocked. We in the Scouts filled straw palliasses for them, and they slept in halls. But they didn't like it, it was too quiet for them. Most of them went back I'd say within a fortnight, although quite a number stayed. Our class had pupils from Glasgow and Edinburgh, and a couple from the east coast, Montrose.

The mixture of people from outside with the natives made it easier. The natives were mostly friendly, but not all of them. It was quite a welcoming community, not organised but individually. A family for example going off on a picnic would invite somebody. A family with children would take along a friend of one of their children, it wasn't because they were an evacuee.

Callander was remote. Unless you were into fishing and running around in the woods, Callander had nothing for you, apart from cinema shows twice a week. I was from a city, but I'd always gone on holidays to farms and I liked it.

Was it an influence on me? Well, I've still an interest in fishing. And I suppose I spent my early teen-age days in the country and then went into agriculture as a career, stemming from that.

There were farmers' children in the school, and some of my friends were farmers' sons, and I went about the farms. Farming was quite small-scale in those days of course. Most things were done by hand. Horses were quite common.

I was fortunate in the people that I was billeted with, really. I was in two other households beyond those I've mentioned, and both were very happy experiences. One family, the father was a postman, he'd been in the services I think. And he was an alpine plant enthusiast, and he had a very substantial collection of alpine plants. In those days there was no such thing as conservation. He used to go up in the hills around Callander collecting plants and I went with him once or twice. I still grow alpines, I think because of the interest I caught from him.

The evacuee experience was very character-forming. You became accustomed to living in other people's homes. You had to attune yourself to how the other family ran things, otherwise there would have been conflict. Most of the evacuees in Callander were on the same basis as me, their billets arranged through their parents. The Glasgow evacuees were another thing. Anyway, it was a curious experience, and I don't really regret it.

c. The Sunday School Picnic, Come Hell or High Water

Dorothy Montgomery, now Mrs. Dorothy Wilson of Dunning, lived in Aberdeen when war broke out.

There were air raids on Aberdeen but as far as I'm aware there was no attempt to mass-evacuate children as there was in Glasgow. I don't know why, because it was quite a strategic point from Norway. We got a lot of raids coming from over that way. Aberdeen had quite a big harbour, and there was Dyce aerodrome. Not a particularly big one, but I think the 621 squadron was based there and they conducted raids on Norway, and I think a lot of propaganda stuff went out from Dyce, dropping leaflets. Then there were a few barracks in Aberdeen, Gordon being the big one.

I can remember vaguely you got a chance at the beginning of the war to put your children to Canada. I can remember my mother and father speaking of that, but at that time Canada was the other end of the world. You had to have someone to sponsor you. My father had cousins over there, but mum just said no, she wouldn't think of it.

To let you understand why I was evacuated: it was one Saturday, the day of the Sunday School picnic, in June 1940. I was nine years old, born the 13th of November, 1930.

My father and my grandfather were both hairdressers. One had a shop at the Bridge of Don, the other a shop in town, in Aberdeen. My job on a Saturday was that I had to take dinner out to them. Saturdays were their busy day and they didn't stop work on those days, they didn't take a dinner hour. First I took my father's, and then I had to rush home and take my grandfather's dinner to him. This day I got to my father's (I took the tram car) and the air raid siren went. Well, there was a Sunday School picnic scheduled for that afternoon, and come hell or high water, I was going to go to this Sunday School picnic.

The tram stopped when the sirens went, so I ran about two miles down to my granny's, picked up my grandfather's dinner, ran to my grandfather's shop, and across a piece of waste ground which was between my grandfather's shop and my house. All this time, apparently, bombs were falling. I wasn't aware of it because I was single-minded, I was going to my Sunday School picnic.

My mother was looking out the window at me coming across this waste ground. And they were machine-gunning the waste ground! My mother went sky-high, and we weren't going to the Sunday School picnic. Well, you can imagine I howled and howled and so we went to the Sunday School picnic. At the picnic the sirens went again and we had to dive into trenches that had been dug up there at Hazelhead Park, and we were all soaked in muddy water.

Well, the result of that was that I cried for days on end, although I thought it hadn't affected me. I can remember running, I can't remember any of the rest of it, you know bombs flying and that, the whole thing was to get to my Sunday School picnic.

The result was that my mother became very concerned that her children were in danger and she evacuated us. She arranged for a friend in Laurencekirk to look after us. It's a town about thirty miles south of Aberdeen. So we went there to live. Unfortunately her best friend hadn't room for us and it was a kind of acquaintance we went to. It was an Englishwoman with two boys, one of an age with my sister and the other younger. My sister was four. At nine, I was the big sister and had to look after her.

Now this is only as seen through the eyes of a child, and probably the woman was all right. But my mother used to send us parcels: I always remember plums, and out of this great big bag of plums we only got two. Her sons got the rest. And there used to be sweets. I don't know if my mother meant them to be divided between the families or not, but we always felt we didn't get our fair share. My sister cried herself to sleep many a time and I had to cuddle her.

The Montgomery family of Aberdeen, 1942:
George, Margaret, Dorothy and Dorothy

I went to school and I enjoyed it and I made a lot of friends there. But I was very unhappy with this woman we stayed with. She didn't misuse us or anything, but she was getting paid for it---my mother did pay her for looking after us. We felt that she had no time for us, and she had time for her sons. But that could have been just a childish thing, that we were unhappy. She wasn't a couthy person. She wasn't somebody like your own mother that would give you a hug when you hurt yourself. It was sort of "Stop your crying". No, not warm. But maybe we were just missing our mum.

I think the little boys took advantage, of getting us into trouble, but maybe not. I always remember one instance. I was that bit older, and my friends were that bit older, and she had one of these sheds that was sloping. There was a wee ladder and we could get up the lower end. We did this and we jumped off the back. It would maybe be only five feet at the back. But to us it was huge. Alan was the oldest boy and we told him we didn't want him to play with us. But he got up there. I can still remember him walking backwards and saying "Ha, ha, ha, I'm up here" and of course he walked too far backward and fell off the higher end. I don't know whether he cut his teeth or bled his nose but there was blood. So we all got a tremendous row for that. We felt, well, it wasn't our fault, because we didn't ask him to go up. (laughs)

I think it was just before Christmas, mum came up, she had come before on weekends, and she took us back and that was the end of me being an evacuee.

When I came back to Aberdeen, I had a friend who was five foot three and she got extra clothes coupons for her height. She was big, you see, for a primary school child. There were only so many shelters for the children, and our schoolroom was above the gym so we went into the gym to get shelter. And we each had to pick a form to lie under, a bench. Mary...the forms were about five feet so if her head was covered her feet were out. So they kept on "Get your feet in." Then "Get your head in." So Mary was finally relegated to behind the piano because there was no form big enough for her.

Aberdeen was the most bombed city in Scotland. It didn't get the worst bombing, because Clydebank had that. But Aberdeen was bombed more often than any other Scottish city, and they had quite a lot of fatalities.

My father was regimental hairdresser to the Gordon Barracks. He had a shop beside the Gordon barracks, which were struck by bombs. Dad was away to the war by then so it was after 1942. Aberdeen had a bad raid and there was lots of damage done. A bomb landed on the NAAFI when there was a dance in progress so there were a lot of people killed.

The blast also damaged my father's shop. I've always been a very independent person and my mother was one of those "Oh, I can't fix a light bulb, oh dear me" people. So when this happened my mother sent me out to see what the shop was like. The door had always been stiff. I turned the handle and pushed the door. There was no glass and I went flying through the door. All the Brylcreem, well it wasn't Brylcreem, it was home-made stuff, all the bottles had shattered, and the stuff was running down the shelves.

That same raid, they also dropped a bomb on Fonthill Barracks. We happened to be visiting some people close by and when the sirens went we all had to run down to the shelter. There was a grocer's shop beside them which used their back garden just for putting out rubbish. It just so happened that a whole pile of wooden orange boxes was there and as we made for the shelter, the bomb dropped. It was a wee bit away, but the blast hit these boxes and they all came tumbling down. It was worse than the bomb blast. Oh, I remember my mother screaming, she thought the bomb had landed about at our feet.

135

No, we weren't in the shelter, but you see children don't worry about these things. It was great fun to us. I can remember being in our shelter and saying "Oh, it's after half past ten. And the all-clear hasn't gone. That means we don't have to go to school till afternoon. And if the all-clear came before half-past ten, "Ahh, dear!" That was the extent that the war affected us.

Chapter 17: BEGGING IN WALES

*Ted Dorsett now lives in Dunning. When World War II broke out,
Ted was a child in London's East End.*

I was born on the June fourteenth, 1937. My first memory is of when we were bombed out of our home. I'm not sure of the year, but it was before I started school. We lived in Lewisham, a place called Ladywell, in south-east London. We were living not far from a railway junction, so that would have been the target for bombing raids. I was the first of what was to be a family of ten children.

*Mrs. Gwendoline Dorsett, with sons John in pram and Ted
with ice cream, London, 1940*

When air raids occurred we were packed into an Anderson air raid shelter in the back-garden. The adults slept on the floor, probably with some bedding. The other children and I were sleeping on planks, laid the width of the shelter and resting on top of the concrete walls. An air raid occurred in the middle of the night. There was a lot of noise, it was frightening. There were a few loud explosions. We and the planks we were lying on fell on top of the adults. But we couldn't get out because there was an air raid going on

That morning, when the all clear sounded and we left the shelter, we found our house in ruins. Some of the walls were still standing. I do remember my mother managed to cook us breakfast on the old iron range in the kitchen. Then we tried to salvage some bits and pieces, while my father went off to find us some place to live. When he came back he arrived with a horse and cart and an address to which we moved, eight miles away in Grove Park. My father was with us during that bombing, later he joined the army and spent most of his war on the beaches near Dover.

I started school at a primary school called Marble's Lane. I can remember that day and my mother taking me. The next vivid memory I have... I recall being sent home from school around lunchtime on a particular day when the air raid sirens were going. I saw a flight of what I know now were fighter-bombers flying very low across the houses behind the street where I lived. Beyond those houses was a large recreational area and a railway, again with a junction. The planes were thirty or forty feet above the roof tops, you could see the pilots in them. Being a young child, when I saw the pilots in the fighter-bombers naturally I waved, and I remember them waving back to me. They were German fighter-bombers. You could clearly see the swastikas and the insignia of the German air force on these fighters.

I also remember, but I think this also came from conversation after, that we had a large gun emplacement nearby. All the guns were down that day, for what reason we never knew. These fighter-bombers flew over without any reaction from the ground. They flew on and dropped their bombs on the area from which we had moved, and dropped their bombs on the school in Catford. It was lunchtime, the school was filled with pupils and teachers, and there were a lot of deaths. And those same planes, when they'd finished their bombing, strafed the streets of Catford with their machine guns as they flew back. There was a lot of bitterness at the time at the way the people were shot at in the streets.

I can remember several air raids after we moved to Grove Park. When we lived in that house we had an Anderson shelter in the garden and we had what they called a Morrison shelter in the living room. A Morrison shelter is a great thick plate of steel supported by four angle-iron legs, with a wire cage all the way round. The wire cage was really just to protect you from bits falling in if the room collapsed. The idea was that you could be in your home and if it received a hit, and the walls and the ceiling came down, you would be inside this very strong box which was as I remember it double bed size. We used to sleep there. So we'd go there irrespective of whether there was an air raid. It was easier to do that than to get up in the night from an unprotected area and go out into the garden where shrapnel might be falling and then go into an Anderson shelter. I can remember a big bombing raid over the back of us. They missed the nearby railway junction and hit the recreation area, and when I went over afterward there was a crater the size of a football pitch. And it blew our back door off.

Before I was evacuated, I recall that V1 guided missiles or doodle-bugs were already coming over. I can distinctly recall the sound of this buh-buh-buh-buh funny sound, it was a ram jet engine. It was a pilot-less thing, just full of explosives and it used to fly with this buh-buh-buh noise and then suddenly it would start spitting and sputtering. The engine would stop, and then the contraption would glide and swoop. You never knew where it was going to land. On one occasion I can remember seeing my father on a bicycle coming up the street towards us with one of these things pitching around the sky, he not knowing which way to direct his bike. I can remember being thrown into the Anderson shelter when these things were going over. One landed near our house and I can remember playing in the wreckage of one of these V1 things.

There's one other memory that I have concerning the V1 doodle-bugs. And it's also an indication of the free-roaming individual I was when I was young. About a half a mile or a mile from where I lived, there is a place called Sundridge Park golf course. In my younger days, it was a large open hilly area. They've now turned it into a splendid golf course. But it was an open roaming ground for me, with some woods. The Home Guard or the Land Army or some military were in the area because they used to have what we called dungeons. They lived in these concrete bunkers, because the area was an ideal place for a landing to take place during an air raid if agents or saboteurs were going to parachute in.

As a youngster, I used to roam over this area with other youngsters, and I can distinctly remember being frightened one day when aircraft, our fighters, were chasing a doodle-bug to try to machine-gun it down and/or tip it over. And because we were frightened we lay under a hedge, as if that would have given us any protection. We dodged under this hedge while these things flew over. We were just sort of free-roaming spirits really. That was my life as a youngster at home. My mother already had too many children to worry about us.

The next thing that I recall was being packed off as an evacuee. I think ordinarily they sent children away as evacuees when they were five years of age. Whatever the reason, I was at school at five, and I wasn't evacuated until I was about seven and my brother came with me. He's eighteen months younger.

It wouldn't have been possible for my mother to go, because she was continuing to have babies, to help the war effort. There were young sisters. My mother had two batches of children, five and five. While I was away, my sisters were sent away for care, and she went to Somerset to give birth to the youngest of the first batch of five.

My brother and I left home as part of a programme of dispersement of children from that area. We were sent to Wales.

My first memory is of being at the station, dressed in my Sunday best, carrying my little bag of sandwiches and sweets for the day, holding my brother's hand, being with an adult and other children, and with a little gas-mask. Lots and lots of children really. I remember the train journey because when the train went through a tunnel, there were no lights on the train, someone nicked my bag of sweeties and thumped me one. And of course I was crying, we came out to the light of day, and I had no sweeties.

The next thing I remember is being in some sort of assembly area which was either a church hall or a railway waiting room. I think it must have been a church hall near the village in which we were to be billeted. I remember that day dragging on a bit but then to a youngster any time is a long time. Other children were disappearing. Suddenly a young woman of about eighteen to twenty came and took us from this assembly area, and I think things went a bit astray there. I don't think we should have been taken. This young woman did not take us to live with her, but deposited us with her grandparents.

So here were two young city ruffians, if you like, being dumped on an elderly Welsh couple, one of whom was blind or had very poor eyesight. I can remember a great welcoming, and the young lady being there, and our being shown into this house after our journey, and being fed and put to bed, feeling quite strange about it all and quite upset. And I can remember my brother crying himself to sleep that night.

One of the things that went wrong on that first meeting with the people that we were evacuated to was that my brother and I occasionally wet the bed but my brother was still bed-wetting regularly. My mother had given me a piece of rubber sheeting to be sure to tell our new foster-parents or carers that this was to go into the bed before we went to bed, and I forgot to do that. So there was a bed-wetting exercise that night, and that didn't go down well at all and started things off in a bad way, because the bed-wetting didn't stop. Now I can look back and think…well, with all the trauma of what was going on…it was no wonder there was some bed-wetting.

Ted Dorsett, 1944

The elderly couple we were with could not really cope with two young boys who were little buggers, really. We were used to having our own way, doing our own thing, running free whenever we could. They weren't prepared and equipped to handle us, plus the bed-wetting. Relationships deteriorated until in the end, we didn't have a bed to sleep in, we slept on the floor. And my brother's memory, though not mine, is that we had to live under the table in the kitchen in the end.

I know that food didn't come very easily to us. We had to wait until everybody else in the family was fed, even the animals. We were considered two bad little boys. Food got less and less. My brother reminded me recently me that all our clothes, any nice clothes that my mother sent us, were taken away and given to other people around the village. Now I don't particularly remember that. He also reminded me that we stole food from the house we were living in. He reminded me of the occasion when we stole raw liver and sat under this table when the family was in bed eating raw liver.

Because of what happened in the home we were in and the way we began to be treated, we started to pick up food on the streets in order I suppose to survive. If there was an apple core on the street that had something on it, we would pick it up and eat it. My brother and I used to go and steal the miners' pieces, packed lunches, from where they stored them at the pithead. There was a pithead near us. We found out where their rations were and we used to go and take their lunch boxes, and steal things like that. We also used to go into the local baker's shop and steal the cakes from the window. We'd line up in the queue and either my brother or I would slide the glass back whilst the other one helped himself to the cakes. We'd go out of the shop and go with other children up to the hills and eat the spoils of what had been taken. It became a game as well as necessity.

My mother tells me that a neighbour of hers, a Welsh lady that lived in the same street at Grove Park, had been home to Wales so she must have been near to where I was evacuated, because she came back and said to my mother that she had seen me "I saw your Teddy," she said, "at the chip shop asking the man in the chip shop for chips." So that was a little story that came home to my mother. Generally my brother and I would be going into the shops and asking for scraps to be given. We used to get the scraps, but I think they turned against us when we started to take what we couldn't get.

My next recollection of those times is that I got sores: scabies, impetigo or something of that nature. Caused, I think, by these heat bumps you get in the summer. You get a heat bump come up and you scratch it, and then it weeps a bit.

Anyway, I finished my time in Wales in a very sorry state. I had so many scabs on me I couldn't face going to school.

For a period, I just hung around the streets. My brother, remember he was eighteen months younger than me, quite clearly remembers that I ran away and left him behind. I ran away and lived rough, he says. He says that it was a milkman that I used to help sometimes that finally told people where I was, and they picked me up. He said that I was living in an old car, and I distinctly remember an old car that we used to play in, an old wreck of a car which was in an open area at the back of the shops that we used to steal from. He said I was away for several days.

I've since done some calculations and I figure that I was only evacuated for something like six to nine months, probably from the summertime to the following April, a period that included Christmas. It was springtime that I ran away, if that's what I did. I was picked up on the streets in a poor condition and put into what I thought was a hospital, but my brother says, "You went into a home". What I do remember about that place I stayed was that they used to put me in special baths as a matter of routine. After I'd been there what seemed just one or two days, they then collected my brother and he joined me in this home or centre.

My next recollection is of an aunt, not a blood relation but the wife of one of my father's friends, coming to collect and take us back to London.

When I came back to London, the V2s were going. The V2 was a much bigger rocket than the V1 and it travelled at or faster than the speed of sound. You would hear the explosion of the V2 as it hit the ground, and then you would hear it coming, after the explosion. Jokingly, we used to say if you heard the bang, you were okay, you were alive.

My mother really didn't know about our experience, because she was away herself. The few times that I've spoken to her about it, she didn't know that we were having a bad time. We used to write home, we had letters dictated to us. We were told what to write by the people we were with. I don't remember having a sweet whilst I was there. Now I know sweets were scarce but my mother said she used to send us little parcels of things. I don't ever remember receiving a parcel.

I remember a sweet once, but that's it. When I talk to her she asks "But what happened to those things that I sent you?" It's as if I didn't have a family anywhere else, that's my memory.

Photographs for Dad

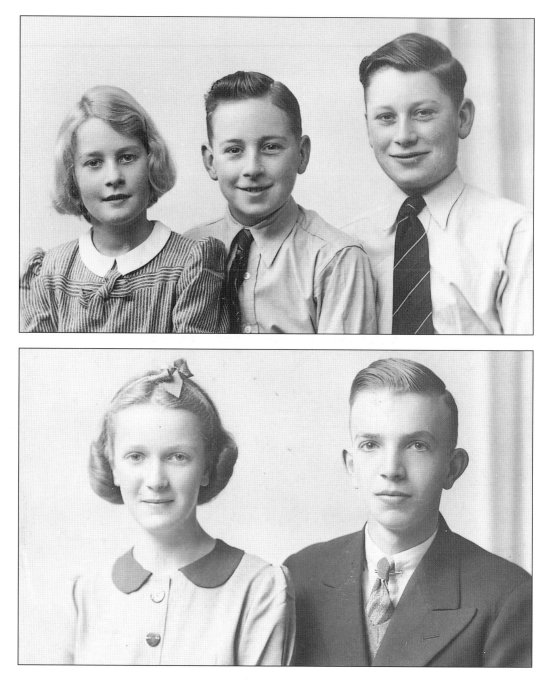

*Film for family cameras was generally unavailable during the war. So, for far-away fathers,
photographs of evacuees were sometimes taken in commercial studios.
These portraits, taken in Perth, are of Glasgow evacuees living in Dunning.
Top: Morag, Eric and Bill Smith. Bottom: Ella and Alex Steel*

Last Memories

The cookery and woodworking classrooms, next to the wee school

Chapter 18: BACK TO DUNNING

We've saved a few varied and poignant recollections about Dunning to conclude. In this chapter we hear from George Boardman, mentioned in the first chapter of this book. George, with Lily (Freeland) King, organised the 1995 evacuee event in which a bronze plaque was placed in Dunning to thank the villagers for taking in World War II evacuees.

I came here the first day of the war. I arrived at the school from the station on a bus. We were all given to different people to stay with. I was aged twelve and I was picked with another five boys to go to Clevage farm on Bridge of Earn Road. The farmers picked big boys, and the idea was to be working on the land, because most of their workers were away to the army.

I only spent one night at the farm, as my mother came and took me back into the village the next morning. My mother had arrived late at night along with Mrs. Freeland, but she could not get out to the farm for me that night.

We both got put up in a lovely little house in Auchterarder Road, which belonged to two sisters named Miss Boag. To me they seemed quite old, but they were very nice ladies. I remember they had a very noisy parrot.

My mother was allowed to stay because she had got a job with Mrs. Freeland looking after the children who were allocated to Mr. and Mrs. McKinnon at the Manse.

I was too old for the Dunning School so I had to go every day with a few other children to Auchterarder School by bus.

After a few months I got an early morning job before school, delivering rolls and milk for Robertson the bakers. Every time now I smell fresh rolls I think of Robertson the baker.

I then got an after school hours job in Angus the butcher's shop in Muckhart Road, mainly scrubbing the counters and keeping the shop clean, also the vans.

I remember once I was told to cycle out to a farm in Auchterarder Road and collect three dead chickens. I wanted to be quick to go and get back, so Mr. Angus would think I didn't waste time. I certainly came back quicker than going, because the farmer's wife just went out and killed the birds, but one came running out with no head on, so I was on the bike like a bullet and back without the birds. Remember I was only twelve years old, I had never seen anything like that before.

My mother and I got a house of our own in Lower Granco Street with the stairs outside looking over the burn, and it was great.

I also joined the Boys Brigade and finished up a sergeant. I loved Dunning and the people, they were all good and kind to me.

I left school and got a full time job in Milne the butcher's, in the square, and I enjoyed it. I learned a lot from George Henderson and especially George Isdale. With three Georges in the shop, we were known as one, two, three. I was George the Third.

When I was working in Milne's I had to clean out the delivery vans. I had always to ask someone in the shop to put them in the garage. But one day, being young, and always wanting to drive, I drove one of the vans into the garage myself, but much to my horror, I smashed it into the back wall.

My mother and I had to move to a house on the ground floor on the Perth Road, for reasons of her health. Then my mother took a heart attack. She was taken to Perth hospital, and sadly died there.

George Boardman at age 16

Mr. Milne, my boss, told me after the funeral in Glasgow that if I wanted to come back to Dunning, which he knew I loved, I could stay with his family in their house, which I did.

Mr. Milne actually wanted to adopt me after my mother died. I was working night and day and he wanted to adopt me because I was a great worker and that. I told my father about it and I said I loved Dunning, and my father said it was up to me. Then I took ill, I was in bed with a poisoned thumb, and the doctor told me to take three days off. Mr. Milne didn't like that. He said if I was going to be in bed, I was no use to him. Me being a young boy and with no mother, and quite headstrong, I just packed my bag and went home to Glasgow.

For Edna Morrison (now Mrs. Robertson of Bishopbriggs), being evacuated wasn't happy, it wasn't unhappy, it was "just something you had to do".

I was born 15th of September, 1932. When war broke out, my father was dead. He had died a year or so previously of tuberculosis, which was a scourge of the time. I had two brothers, Ian, four years older than me, Alex, two years older than me.

Edna Morrison

The whole school, Haghill Primary, was evacuated, and we just went with the school. Half the school went to Dunblane, and half went to Dunning. The train stopped at Dunblane, then went on to Dunning. My brothers must have been told we all had to stay together, which presented problems for village people who might perhaps take me, or they would take the two boys but not the three of us. So I think we were towards the end before the infant mistress, Miss Phillips, and her sister who kept house for her, took the three of us. It was the schoolhouse of the small school at the top of the hill where we stayed with them.

People say the evacuation must have been distressing, but I don't really remember it being very distressing. For my mum, looking back, I don't remember her feelings but as a mother myself she must have been distraught, having her husband die just a short time before and then her three children taken away. She went to work in munitions. Perhaps that was the reason she didn't come with us. Her father was still alive, and he came to stay with her.

We stayed with Miss Phillips a while. I think it went all right with me, but not so much for the boys. The ladies were very strict, and I think the discipline was a bit much. They were both maiden ladies and I don't think they were used to having children staying with them.

We went to stay with Miss Belle Flockhart, who had a shop in the village. That was great fun, we all worked in the shop. She was a great character. She was a Miss, but had two sons, which didn't seem odd to us at the time. And they came back to Dunning from London. They had jobs as waiters or something with the

German Embassy or the Russian Embassy, and of course they were jobless. They came back with a friend Peter, and we had really good fun with them.

Then there were soldiers being billeted in the village and she had to take in soldiers. That's when the younger brother Alex and I went up to the manse and my brother Ian went to Clark's Dairy.

Ian Morrison

The manse was more staid. Miss Flockhart was convinced we'd all starve up there, and we wouldn't be warm enough. She was always shouting "Have you got your Liberty bodice on?" or something like that. It was such an embarrassment… you might be walking down the street! But she was very nice, she was lovely.

At the manse they were very kind. It was more strict, but not unduly. We didn't starve, we didn't freeze. Then the other children there, the three Lothian children and my brother Alex, went back to Glasgow. But Margaret Freeland came to the manse as a maid. She was great, she couldn't have been much older than I was. She was brilliant and she used to sing at the troops' concerts and that. I had great fun with her, she was really nice.

There were buses at one point for mothers to come up. My mother was…this is dreadful…the champion bomb-maker. They had production incentives for whose machines produced the most bombs. And then she actually married the engineer who serviced all the machines, so it was a great joke that he made sure that her machine was the most efficient. She married during the war. We were still evacuated. Yes, it was a shock for us, I suppose, but it turned out all right and his son became a great friend of ours too.

It must do something to you, I suppose, the experiences. But it was just a necessary experience, being evacuated, wasn't it? It wasn't unhappy, it wasn't happy. It was just something you had to do, something you did. I find it quite interesting now when you see George Boardman and Lily Freeland at the reunions, their mothers were with them and that must have made it more rose-coloured. For those who had their mothers, it was more like a big holiday, I suppose. For those of us separated from our mothers, it was different. I don't remember it being unhappy, but I don't remember it being particularly happy, just a time to go through.

I think I was a Glasgow keelie, I could hold my own. I don't remember being intimidated by people, which is a bit of luck. But looking back, it could have been bad. I think if you've come through your father dying and that experience, war starting, you just wonder what it does do to you.

What's a Glasgow keelie? Just a Glaswegian, brash and tough. I suppose Dunning was more posh than where I came from. The East End of Glasgow was not a salubrious area. It wasn't bad, it was clean and tidy and all that, I've got no hang-ups about it. Dunning was different, back and front door. Staying at the manse, looking back on it must have been quite an experience, you know they had their blue room, and their gold room, their yellow room and their pink room.

My mother was dead keen that I should learn to play the piano, and she arranged for me to have music lessons in Perth. I was allowed to go by bus into Perth, but the minister wouldn't allow you to use the piano to practice on. Going to Perth was a good skive because you got away from school, and I don't think I even bothered going to the lessons half the time, but I just had a good time in Perth. I don't think I would have been a pianist anyway, but the minister didn't encourage you, not letting you use the piano. But it would have been nice to try. My mother got a piano when I got back from Dunning and that was supposed to be the big treat. But I completed ignored the piano and went for the piano stool, which I still have. My mother's hopes for my musical talents were never fulfilled.

May McDermott (now Mrs. Cameron) came to Dunning with her mother and her younger brothers Morris and Richard. Mother and daughter went back to Glasgow after a year, the boys stayed longer. May and Richard tell about it:

May: The people we were billeted with were tenant farmers and we thought it exciting to live on, as we thought, a farm. It was really a small dairy at the edge of the village. We were delighted to be able to roam in the fields where there were cows, and to be allowed to feed the chickens in the backyard. The farmer's wife milked the cows by hand and we marvelled at how quickly and deftly her fingers worked as the milk squirted into the pail.

We also found it strange to get used to oil lamps for lighting as there was no electricity in the house then. So no wireless or radio! Also if you went along to the baker's shop for bread you had to ask for half a loaf if you only wanted one! Otherwise you would have been given two if you asked for a loaf. Very strange! Though I do believe there are some parts of Scotland where they still do that even today.

In those days Dunning boasted two bakers' shops and one fish and chip shop. Some things I recall are long walks, picnics in the Dragon and on the banks of the Burn. Picking brambles for Mum to make jam (though sugar was rationed and my Mum could not make a lot). We caught trout in the Burn. That was great fun. Going to the "witch's cairn" where a poor unfortunate woman Maggie Walls was burned on the spot in 1657. Visits to Perth and Auchterarder. Most of my memories are happy ones.

We returned to Glasgow after a year or so as my mother went to work in Beardmore's munitions factory. My father was in the army and the allowance was not a lot. Most people were not well off in those days.

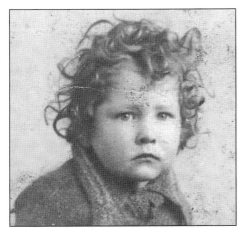

Richard McDermott

Richard McDermott: My first primary school was here. I can just remember learning the alphabet. It was nearly all Glasgow children. The Glasgow kids, we used to go together, have snow fights with the local children. We actually fitted in with the local kids, but kids of course gang up together.

As kids we went pinching apples from the headmaster's garden. Eating them, I remember that.

My father was in the war, he eventually was wounded and came home to hospital in 1945. My mother and sister, they stayed in Glasgow during the war, though my mother died seven months before the war ended.

When my father got some leave, he and my mother would come up to visit us. That was one of the things, my mother was the talk of the town, because my father took my mother into a pub with the kids. She only drank lemonade, and so did the kids, but she was still the talk of the town. (laughs) A scandal!

May: My mum decided one day, let's go through and see the boys. They were staying at the farm in Dunning. We went down unannounced. They weren't in when we arrived, all the children were out playing.

We sat waiting for them coming in, and when they came in, we were shocked at the condition they were in. They were very pale and sort of undernourished-looking, not very clean, raggedy-looking.

Mum was horrified. She decided then she would take them home. Their hair was dirty and verminous. It really was disgusting. We assumed the other evacuee children who were staying there in the same house must have been in the same condition. So mum got them home to Glasgow, and back to normal.

One reason my mother had decided earlier to go back to Glasgow with me was because she didn't feel well in Dunning. She felt maybe the bracing air was causing it. Actually, she had a heart condition.

The parents: Mrs. Mary McDermott and John McDermott
photographed at the outbreak of World War II.
He was called up a week before the war, and is still wearing
the old uniform he had worn in World War I.

My father was in the Engineers, and he was wounded in Germany building a bridge across the Rhine. He came back on a troop train to a hospital in Glasgow, and sent word to us. My brother Morris and I went to see him, and he immediately asked "Where's your mother?" We had to tell him she was not well enough to come. She died just a fortnight later.

Marian Inglis (now Mrs. Leah of Leeds) was an infant when she came to Dunning with her family. Her memories are fragmentary, but she has some strongly held views about the evacuation.

I came to Dunning in 1941 when I was three with my cousin and her mother, and my brother and my mother. The fathers of the two families stayed in Glasgow to work. We didn't come with a school evacuee group, we came independently and rented a flat.

It was a very pleasant experience coming here, but of course we came with our mothers and we also saw our fathers so it wasn't really a separation as such. It wasn't like the evacuees who came and didn't know whether they would see their parents again or not.

We only stayed two years, but even though I was small, we had lots of pleasant memories. Though I didn't take part, I can remember being taken along to the tattie howking. Eventually I did go to the little school up the hill, perhaps for just two or three months.

I've heard the evacuees at the reunions talk about their experiences, but ours were completely different. It was because we came with our family, and there was no split. I should imagine some of the evacuees were traumatised for life, quite frankly, depending on who they met.

Lloyd and Marian Inglis

It was what I would call politics choosing a strategy for the war effort. They hadn't really thought it through at all. All they wanted was the children out of the way so there'd be a future generation. The government didn't realise how much scarring might occur.

The Polly, Dunning Burn

Chapter 19: THE RUNAWAYS

On September 3, 1995, a year after the first Dunning evacuees' reunion, the evacuees held a special event in the village. They unveiled a plaque thanking the villagers for their kindness to them as youngsters.
The event was well-advertised in advance.

When Mrs. May Reid of Bishopbriggs saw the publicity, she obtained special permission to leave the cancer ward of a Glasgow hospital to attend the event with her brother Ken Purdon of Kirkintilloch.
That afternoon, they recorded this interview.

Ken Purdon and May (Purdon) Reid, Dunning, September 3, 1995

Ken Purdon: We were from Balornock, Glasgow, in the Springburn area, north of the city. We were evacuated twice. The first time we went to Ellon in Aberdeenshire, and then they brought us all home again. When the Clydebank blitz started, they moved us again and we came to Dunning.

May (Purdon) Reid: The first time more or less the whole of Balornock school was evacuated. It was a great adventure for us. We were at the station when somebody came and said war was declared. It was a very long journey, taking the route around the Firth of Forth. There was an air raid alert which turned out to be false, but they stopped the train with hundreds of children just prior to the Forth Bridge. The plane that came over turned out to be a reconnaissance plane.

157

Ken: They thought they were going to attack the Forth Bridge. We sat there for about two hours, staying on the train.

May: We arrived very late at night. We'd been travelling since nine o'clock in the morning. We were herded into a school, and people came in and chose who they were going to take. My sister Winnie was with us that time. We were eventually sent out to a farm very far out of Ellon.

At the end of three months my mother came up and took us home. There'd been no raids and it really wasn't a right war at that point. I don't remember very much about that evacuation.

The evacuation that sticks in my mind is the second one, after the Blitz started. A house just around the corner from our home was bombed. Everybody was panic-stricken, and all the children were getting sent away again. We were sent to Dunning. There were maybe fifty of us from different schools in our area on the train but there weren't very many came to Dunning.

Ken: This time there was just the two of us.

May: I was eleven and my brother was seven.

Ken: We were taken up to the manse, and people came from the farms and from the village to pick who they were taking. We were taken by a family from a farm up the road. It turned out to be an unfortunate experience. They had two boys, and the older one gave us a very hard time when we were there. He was about thirteen or fourteen, and he was a sadistic type of boy.

We've heard since he turned out mentally ill. We were back at the farm today and the lady who has the farm showed us through it. We saw the place where our bedroom was, just off the kitchen.

We weren't allowed into the main house. There was a door off the kitchen into this small bedroom, which just held a bed. That was ours, the two of us. If we wanted a toilet there was an outside toilet in the yard. The only time we were allowed into the main house was on a Friday night for a bath. The first door on the left was the bathroom and that's as far as we ever got.

May: We didn't eat with the family. We had tea separately. And we were kept very much apart from the family. This boy…I realise now he was probably a bit mentally unstable then…the worst thing that I remember about him is that he had little capsules of some chemical they used for the sheep dip. He used to cut the tops off and spray them on the back of my legs and I used to come out in big burned blisters.

And his mother wouldn't believe me. The blisters were there for her to see and the burns were there and she wouldn't believe that her son had done this. It got so bad that when he did it again I was frightened to tell her and I was frightened to do anything about it. For some reason I was frightened to write home and tell my mother. Probably because his mother hadn't believed me and I thought nobody else would.

My mother used to send us a 1/6d postal order each week for pocket money between us. That was a lot then. I decided that enough was enough, and I was going to try to go home. I started saving up some of the 1/6d. There was a shepherd's cottage up the hill. We used to go up to this cottage and the lady there was very nice to us. I told her I was going to go home, and she found out where I could get a bus. We'd never been on a bus on our own in our life.

The family used to go once a month on a Tuesday to the cattle market in Perth. The whole family went and we were left. So we planned…well, I planned, Ken was too wee…and saved up the money. When I saw they were away to market, we went back for our stuff and away we went. We walked from the farm along to the station road, past the station, to the main road and waited there for a bus home to Glasgow. It took us a very long time to walk that road, and we had to wait a long time for the bus. And so we eventually arrived in the centre of Glasgow. I had the keys, and he had a train under his arm. We didn't leave a note. Nothing.

Ken: And they didn't make any enquiries about where we were, where we went.

May: They didn't do anything about it. My mother of course went to the school and I suppose they informed the family we were home. But they made no contact. The school in Dunning didn't enquire either. My mother almost had a heart attack when she opened the door and we were standing there

Ken: We were there roughly a year because I can recall the cold winter there and the heat of summer there. A year at least.

May: It was during the summer holidays that we left to go home, I know that. We went to the wee school up the hill. Miss Phillip was the teacher.

Ken: I can't recall my teacher's name. But I recall the class being divided by a curtain. There was a class one side of the curtain and a class the other side of the curtain because it was so crowded.

May: Looking back, what do I think of the experience? Well, I was saying to my brother today I've sort of laid a ghost. Because all my life I've had this... more or less a hatred for this boy...and now I realise he was mentally unstable. I think it has been good for me, really. I've never forgotten the details of this boy; I can picture his face to this minute.

Ken: The other boy was fine. The father was very, very quiet.

May: He never had anything to do with us. The mother was a very strict lady. I can picture her face too. And when I went to her about her son, she was so angry with me for saying that her son had done this to me.

This wasn't the only nasty thing her did. We had this outside loo, this dry toilet place that we had to use. And he locked it. Every time he saw me going in he'd lock it from the outside and I couldn't get out, no matter how much I cried or kicked the door or whatever I did. And one day their uncle, who was a nice man...

Ken: He'd got a brand new car which was unusual in time of war, because there were no cars being produced. When he came into the yard he parked it right across the door of this toilet. May had been locked in by the boy.

May: I was in there for hours.

Ken: Eventually she kicked the door open and damaged the car. She got into trouble for that.

May: That's another horror story, that privy.

Ken: We went to bed at nine. This wee room we were in, off the kitchen, had a window into the garden. And the boy used to come to this window when we were in bed and make noises and frighten us. I mean, it sounds silly now but at that age and in a strange place, no parents, it was frightening.

May: We used to lie and sing songs to one another, didn't we? To cheer us along, keep us happy. What songs? "I Got Sixpence, Jolly Jolly Sixpence" and "Show Me the Way to go Home". (laughs) That was our main one. But what it did for us, it created a very close bond between my brother and me. We've always been very close since then, you know.

Ken: We've been the two closest in our family, all these years.

May: So it worked out for good in the end. And I just thought you would like to know about it.

Ken: Mind you, there were good memories too. I had a friend who went to the same school and I got very friendly with him and I used to go to his place.

Another memory: I used to go to school in the afternoons, there was no morning class, and when I came out of the farm going to school, there was this chap who stopped every day and picked me up. He was a telephone engineer, and he drove a wee green telephone van. If I wasn't there, he'd stop and wait till I came out. Kindnesses like that, you remember.

May: I went to school in the morning. The farmer used to run his sons into school every morning, and I walked. We weren't allowed in the car at all.

Ken: He had a beautiful big car, I remember, which he used to drive extremely slowly. It was like a funeral going by. The local kids used to make jokes of it. We weren't allowed in the car, just as we weren't allowed in the house: only the once a week, through this door into the main house and the bath was right there. That was as far as we ever got.

May: We were only allowed in the farm kitchen or this wee tiny bedroom. We ate by ourselves. They had a big woman worked for them, and she used to put our meals in front of us, but nobody ate with us. I did have a good friend, Margaret Freeland, and her mother was very kind to me, and I used to go up to their house with Margaret, and they were very nice to me.

Ken: The shepherd's wife up the hill, too, she was very good to us. She had a family of her own, two boys and a girl, and we went up there regularly.

May: This has been a catharsis, this trip. I actually should be in the hospital, but I asked to get out today to come here. Because I wouldn't have missed it for anything. It has been marvellous, wonderful.

Ken: The other evacuees we've been talking to at the reunion were well-treated, very well-treated. I guess it's just the luck of who you landed with, you know.

Ken Purdon and May (Purdon) Reid in Dunning, September 3, 1995

**Mrs. May (Purdon) Reid died on February 20, 1996,
five months after this return journey to Dunning.**

The relationship between the village of Dunning, Perthshire, and its World War II evacuees continues. On September 3, 1999, the sixtieth anniversary of the mass evacuee arrival was marked by a day long reunion, with school visits, village tours, a reception by the Dunning Parish Historical Society and a big band dance featuring music of the wartime period. Participating were a good number of evacuees (coming from as far away as France), villagers, and present-day pupils of both Haghill and Dunning Primary Schools.